GOLDEN YEARS OF
PRO
FOOTBALL

GOLDEN YEARS OF PRO FOOTBALL

JIM CAMPBELL

Crescent Books

New York/Avenel, New Jersey

This 1993 edition published by Crescent Books, distributed by Outlet Book Company, Inc., a Random House Company, 40 Engelhard Avenue Avenel, New Jersey 07001

Produced by Brompton Books Corporation 15 Sherwood Place Greenwich, CT 06830

ISBN 0-517-06978-4

8 7 6 5 4 3 2 1

Printed in Slovenia

To my parents, Howard and Evelyn Campbell, who always encouraged my "improbable dream."

To my wife Brenda, who was a bigger help than she'll ever know.

To others too numerous to mention, but we both know who you are and what you've done.

Page 1: *Jubilant Cleveland Browns celebrate their 1954 NFL title after downing the Detroit Lions, 56-10.*

Page 2: *The 49ers' ace quarterback Joe Montana, considered by some as the best quarterback ever, led his team to four Super Bowl victories during the eighties.*

Right: *Green Bay Packers quarterback Bart Starr (15) watches as teammate Jim Taylor powers into the end zone during Super Bowl I.*

CONTENTS

The 1958 sudden death National Football League Championship Game between the New York Giants and Baltimore Colts was proclaimed "The Greatest Game Ever Played." At the time, there were doubters – the game's participants among them. Today, there seem to be even more Thomases to cast doubt on applying "the Greatest" to that landmark contest.

True, the Colts' 23-17 overtime sudden death victory could hardly compare in skill and execution to games played later – or to the overall level of play in today's NFL – but for impact, drama and symbolism this game can arguably still be called "the Greatest." And what it did to raise the football consciousness of the American sporting public can never be minimized.

There has been football in the United States since the mid-1800s. There has been professional football since the Gay Nineties (1892). But from its formative years, pro football was almost a cult sport, followed by relatively few fans in one region of the nation, the Northeast.

The NFL, when it stabilized in the 1940s, existed in nine northern cities – none farther west than Chicago; none farther south than Washington, DC. The sport of pro football trailed both major league baseball and college football in fan interest and appeal and may have even been fourth to boxing's following.

The 1958 NFL championship game, set in New York – which had just recently awakened to the glamor of the NFL – captured a nation's fancy and turned a game into a Sunday ritual, a mass cult sport with a tremendous following. Pro football became a topic of conversation and a cause for celebration!

That the Giants of New York – with Charlie Conerly, Frank Gifford, Sam Huff and Andy Robustelli – were contending for NFL supremacy and that Madison Avenue's advertising industry and the television networks were becoming aware of the NFL and its players as marketing tools, certainly didn't hamper pro football's national acceptance. As the Madison Ave boys might have said about pro football, "Let's run it up the flagpole and see who salutes it." Well, a vast number of Americans clicked their collective heels and "saluted it."

Pro football and television had been paired up as far back as the late 1930s, when NBC televised a Brooklyn Dodgers vs. Philadelphia Eagles game on October 22, 1939, to the handful of TV receivers located in the metropolitan New York area. But nothing spurred on the pro game like network, coast-to-coast, weekly coverage of the NFL.

Television can be said to have hurt the appeal of boxing by overexposure in the mid-1950s. But when TV brought the NFL into America's living rooms, it created a whole new public – fans who never had even thought about attending a pro football game. What TV did for pro football in the beginning of extended coverage was to bring the speed and power of the runners, the violence and strength of the linemen, and the grace and skill of passers and receivers right to you in the comfort of your own home. If ever a couple was suited for marriage, it was the NFL and TV in the fifties.

In many ways, the NFL/TV marriage is still on an extended honeymoon. TV provides the NFL worldwide exposure, but the NFL provides TV a dramatic offering of which the public in ever-increasing numbers can't seem to get enough. As other sports activities vie for the American entertainment dollar, NFL football has become the single most popular sport in the nation, according to Harris polls taking into account the number of people who follow the sport.

While this volume focuses on the golden years of pro football from 1946 to the present, an overview of the sport's history is important to place the modern game in perspective. The worldwide acceptance of pro football today belies its humble beginnings. Pro football was indeed the stepchild of American sports in its infancy. So little attention was paid to the origins of the game that for many years the true story of where and when it began was erroneously reported. In fact, in some unenlightened accounts it is still wrongly noted.

Dr. John Brallier of Latrobe, Pennsylvania, declared himself the first professional football player, years after the fact, when he came forth and admitted to taking "ten-dollars and 'cakes' [expenses]" for playing for the

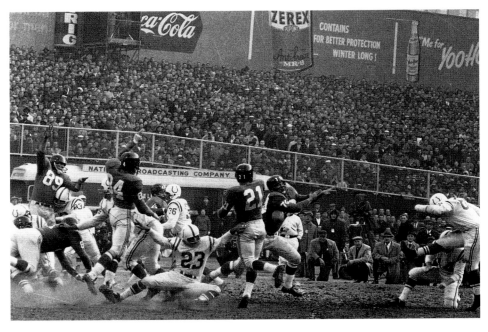

Pages 6-7: *The dynamic action of this L.A. Raiders vs. Denver Broncos game – Roger Craig with the ball – is typical of the "controlled violence" that draws so many to NFL football.*

Left: *Sam Huff (70) of the New York Giants smashes through to block Steve Myhra's field goal attempt in the fabled 1958 sudden death NFL Championship Game, also known as "the Greatest Game Ever Played."*

Opposite: *Although Latrobe, Pennsylvania, was not "the birthplace of pro football," by 1897 all players on the team were paid something for playing – making it the first "all pro" team.*

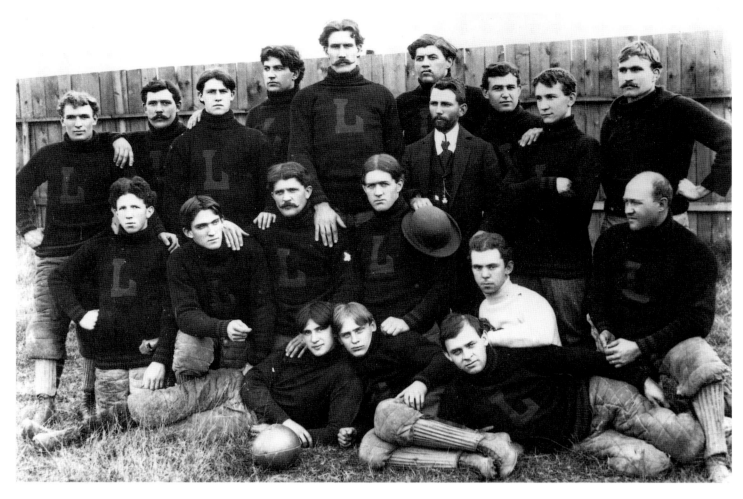

Latrobe YMCA-sponsored team against a neighboring Western Pennsylvania town team from Jeannette. At the time, the payout was kept very quiet. Because of Brallier's declaration, "Latrobe in 1895" was misused as the starting point of pro football.

In the early 1890s, heated rivalries sprang up between the athletic clubs of Pittsburgh. One of the hottest involved the Pittsburgh Athletic Club (PAC) and the Allegheny Athletic Association (AAA). To assure victory, the AAA recruited former Yale All-America guard William "Pudge" Heffelfinger. Although Heffelfinger was a lifelong outspoken critic of the pro game and denied ever "playing for pay," there is no doubt that the redoubtable Pudge was a hired hand. A yellowed page from an Allegheny Athletic Association ledgerbook has this telltale entry: *W. Heffelfinger for playing (cash) – $500.* Heffelfinger may have been a bargain. He won the game – which featured heavy betting by backers of both clubs – by causing a fumble with a jarring tackle, picking up the loose ball, and returning it to score the game's only and winning touchdown. The date of the entry was November 12, 1892. Other Ivy League gentlemen were employed during that era, though not at the *per diem* of Heffelfinger. Among the early pros – earlier by several years than Brallier – were Ed Malley, Ben (Sport) Donnelly, Knowlton (Snake) Ames and Lawson Fiscus.

While Latrobe cannot rightfully claim the first pro player, it can claim to have had the first pro team. The 1897 Latrobe team, managed by newspaperman Dave Berry, was made up entirely of players who each received some fee for playing each game. Pro football flourished in Western Pennsylvania through the Gay Nineties and into the early twentieth century, but by 1904 the seat of power was shifting westward to Ohio. The Buckeye State had no less than eight acknowledged pro teams, and those in the Pittsburgh district were in decline because of Pennsylvania "blue laws" that prohibited Sunday athletic competition.

The hotbed of Ohio pro football centered in Canton, Massillon and Akron. To gain the edge, the best talent was imported by the local teams. Many Pennsylvania stars were recruited in the beginning, but in 1915 one name stood above all the rest – Jim Thorpe. The fabled Carlisle All-America halfback and 1912 Olympic pentathlon and decathlon winner was brought by team manager Jack Cusack to play for the Canton Bulldogs. Thorpe was unquestionably the biggest name to play pro football at the time, and the game's largest drawing card.

The Ohio teams played each other and other pro teams mostly from the Midwest, though they did not exist within an organized league. The matter of a formal league was taken care of on September 17, 1920, when representatives from the leading pro teams met in Canton in Ralph Hay's Hupmobile and Jordan automobile agency to form the American Professional Football Association. Thorpe was named president of the newly-formed league, but after a year as figurehead, the leadership of the league was assumed by newspaperman-turned-sports-manager, Joe Carr.

Among those on hand at the start of the league, which would change its name to the National Football League in 1922, was George Halas, recently of the University of

Illinois and the organizer of a company team for the Staley Starch Works of Decatur, Illinois. Halas was not, as later depicted, *the* founder of the NFL, but one of several founders. Representatives of 10 other teams shared space on the Jordan and Hupmobile running boards with Halas that sweltering Friday evening.

While pro football was looked down upon, as were most "pro" sports, the post-graduate game of football was beginning to develop a following in the 1920s. Mostly blue-collar types – men who had no alma mater – followed the local pro team. Stadiums and playing fields were small, thus crowds were relatively small, too. But the pro game aroused interest in certain circles.

Two things happened in 1925 to change the face of pro football. First, Tim Mara invested in a New York NFL franchise – called the Giants after their landlords and baseball counterparts. Next, Red Grange turned pro after his last college game at Illinois. Grange, his manager Charles C. ("Cash and Carry") Pyle, and George Halas arranged a coast-to-coast barnstorming tour that was to begin with a game between Halas's team – by then playing in Chicago and known as the Chicago Bears – and the cross-town rival Chicago Cardinals. The tour, seven games in 11 days in such cities as St. Louis, Philadelphia, New York and Boston, drew large crowds – including an overflow throng of 70,000 at New York's Polo Grounds – and brought pro football to where it had never been before. Grange, the most publicized athlete the country would see until the modern mass-media era, was like the Pied Piper of Football. He, almost single-handedly, brought people out to see the game on the magic of his name. The tour went through the South and concluded on the West Coast.

Once New York had a franchise, economics and geography combined to move the NFL from the mid-sized cities of the Midwest to the larger metropolitan areas. The Dayton (Ohio) franchise transferred to Brooklyn. Pottsville (Pennsylvania) relocated in Boston. Rock Island (Illinois), Columbus (Ohio), Kenosha (Wisconsin) and similar towns dropped out of the NFL. Some were replaced. Others weren't. The only "town team" to survive was the Green Bay Packers. By the 1930s, Pittsburgh, Philadelphia, Detroit, Cleveland and Washington were NFL cities.

As the league evolved, so, too, did the player. In the early years, a pro was someone with a year or two of football he needed to get out of his system, or a "tramp" athlete who just couldn't give up the game. Pro football was not a career. It was truly a sideline. But by the thirties and forties, pros were playing longer and taking the game more seriously. Yes, players still needed to hold off-season jobs and came to camp to "play themselves into shape." But, perhaps because of the Great Depression and the fact that pro athletes were always paid better than the average forest ranger, they began to realize that if pro football wasn't a career in itself, it could be a stepping stone to a solid post-playing career. The average career lengthened and the skill of the average player increased.

Clarke Hinkle placed the pre-World War II NFL in perspective when he said, "We didn't have TV or wide national attention, but we did play a good brand of ball that could, and would, fill a 50,000-seat stadium." While some teams struggled – on the field and at the box office – there was a certain stability and uniformity to the NFL by this time.

Opposite left: *In 1969 Joe Namath of the New York Jets, with his rebel image and unconformist approach to football, gave a whole new constituency of pro football fans a hero with which to identify. Namath probably made more casual observers into rabid fans than anyone in his era. Guaranteeing victory in Super Bowl III did not hinder his becoming an almost mythical character.*

Opposite right: *O. J. Simpson brought the plight of college football's top player to the public's attention. Many were outraged that he, as the Heisman Trophy winner, had no choice after being drafted by "the worst team" – the Buffalo Bills. The draft worked that way – the last shall be first – for years, but hardly anyone cared until a California kid was banished to western New York State's Niagara frontier.*

Right: *Roger Staubach (12) was "the American hero" for "America's team" – the Dallas Cowboys of the 1970s.*

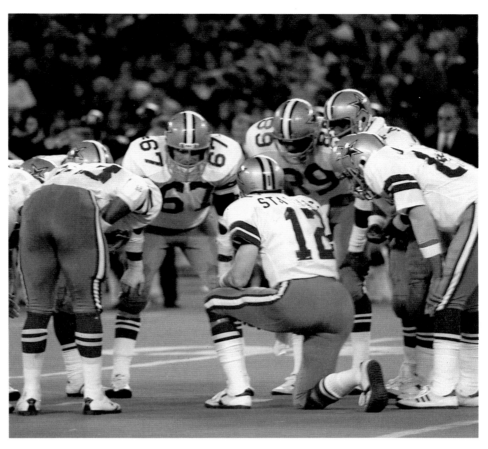

All NFL teams were in either the Eastern or Western division. Each team played the same number of games for the first time, roster limits were adhered to and contracts were honored – no jumping from team to team, week to week.

Pearl Harbor changed America – and the NFL. Players "went off to war." A manpower shortage forced the Cleveland Rams to suspend operations and the Eagles and Steelers to merge into the "Steagles" in 1943. The Steelers then combined with the Cardinals in 1944. But the NFL survived the global conflict, and a new challenge was on the horizon.

While no one could foresee what the NFL would be today, by the end of World War II it had already moved far beyond the ragtag, small town operation that it was in the beginning. The NFL would go through many growing pains and many triumphs, both on and off the field, in the decades to come. The postwar years brought a boom in football's popularity. The fledgling AAFC, starring Paul Brown and his invincible Cleveland Browns, lasted from 1946 through 1949 before merging with the NFL. Pro football went national in 1946, with the Los Angeles Rams locating on the West Coast. And the forties also brought integration, with the breaking of the "colorline" in 1946.

The fabulous fifties saw pro football, aided by television coverage and a high level of player talent, soar in popularity. And it didn't hurt that the 1958 Colts-Giants NFL Championship game went into sudden death overtime, epitomizing the glory and excitement of the gridiron sport.

NFL football had become such a hot prospect that, by the sixties, others wanted to jump on the bandwagon, and the rival AFL was formed. This, together with NFL expansion, spread pro football franchises across the nation. The leagues merged in 1966, but the real news for fans was on the playing fields, where the likes of Johnny Unitas, Joe Namath, Jim Brown and Gale Sayers were rewriting the record books, and the likes of Vince Lombardi's Green Bay Packers were tearing up the turf, winning five NFL Championships and the first two Super Bowls.

The magic continued into the seventies, when Don Shula's Miami Dolphins, Tom Landry's Dallas Cowboys and Chuck Noll's Pittsburgh Steelers stepped into the limelight as dynasty teams. The league reorganized and expanded, and a new American institution was created – "Monday Night Football." Franco Harris, with his "Immaculate Reception" in the '72 playoff, was just one of the many players of the decade whose name became a household word. Others were George Blanda, O.J. Simpson, Tony Dorsett, Earl Campbell, Joe Greene, Ken Stabler, Roger Staubach and Lynn Swann.

The NFL of the eighties can best be described as a "league on the move." With franchise moves, the coming and going of the USFL, and player strikes in '82 and '87, the NFL had its hands full off the field. But great things were happening on the field, beginning with the dramatic San Diego vs. Miami overtime playoff in 1982. Piloted by superstar quarterback Joe Montana, the San Francisco 49ers dominated the league.

The momentum of the eighties continued for pro football into the nineties, as the World League began play in the spring of '91, bringing hometown teams across the globe. Back in the U.S., young stars and future greats toil side by side with crafty veterans, continuing the tradition of excellence and excitement that has become the hallmark of pro football.

1946-1949

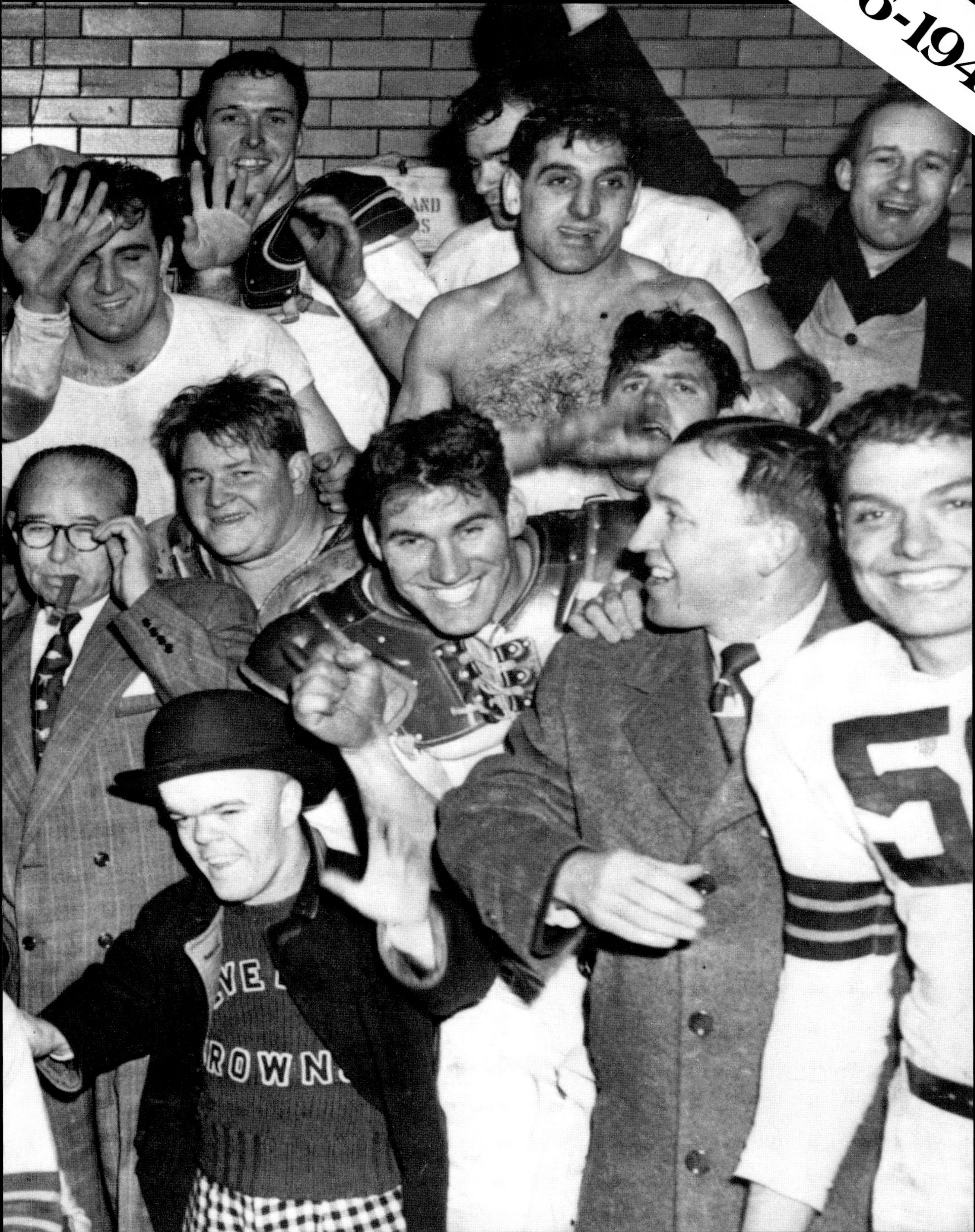

The period of the late forties became known in history as "the post-war boom." Pro football in 1946 was "booming" too. The NFL was thriving when an idea, whose time had come in 1944, was organized in 1945, and put on the playing field a year later. The All-America Football Conference (AAFC) began to play – and to challenge the NFL – in 1946.

The idea of the new league came from the fertile mind of Chicago sportswriter Arch Ward. He felt the country was ready to support more than just a handful of pro teams in the Northeast. He brought together interested parties, and it was decided that with the war over, 1946 would be the year to begin on-field operations.

The NFL, with its own internal concerns, didn't seem too worried about the new kid on the block. In fact, the commissioner of the NFL – old Notre Dame Four Horsemen fullback Elmer Layden – was widely quoted as saying, "First, let them get a football."

The NFL had its own concerns. After coming back for the 1944 season, the Cleveland Rams won the 1945 NFL Championship, led by rookie quarterback and future Hall of Famer Bob Waterfield. But, following a plan of owner Dan Reeves that was conceived before the war, the Rams pulled up stakes and moved to California. They would begin play in 1946 as the Los Angeles Rams – the first major league professional team to locate on the West Coast. When Reeves came up with his idea of western expansion, it is unlikely he thought he would have immediate neighbors. However, California was not to be exclusively NFL territory.

Taking Commissioner Layden's advice, Paul Brown and his All-America Football Conference buddies did get themselves a football – and a little more. The new league located in eight coast-to-coast cities, including three NFL cities – Chicago, Los Angeles and New York – and two California cities (San Francisco and the aforementioned Los Angeles).

Although only four teams from the AAFC would survive a future merger, the newer league was a viable major league with its own cities, own traditional rivalries, and its own home-grown stars.

Cleveland and Paul Brown were by far the success stories of the AAFC. A strong case can be made for the Cleveland Browns actually causing the demise of the "All-American," as it was sometimes called by its players, coaches and fans. The Browns won all four championships the league had, from 1946 through 1949. They were so far ahead of the pack, and Brown's coaching tactics so advanced, that the rest of the league was really only fighting to see who was second-best to the Browns. The AAFC's New York Yankees and San Francisco 49ers were excellent teams, but when it came time for the league's championship games, neither could challenge the Browns' supremacy – nor could anyone else. As the lopsided affair continued, fan interest in the new league began to wane.

With the war over, many good players were available. The NFL couldn't monopolize player talent. New franchises in new cities meant that pro football had finally gone national. Pro football was being played, seen and enjoyed in parts of the country that had only read and heard about it before.

In the war between the AAFC and the NFL for player talent, the players themselves were the big winners, and the team owners were, literally in most cases, the big losers. Salaries escalated as top players had options for the first time. More than one star – Glenn Dobbs and Arnie Weinmeister among them – played three ends (NFL, AAFC and the Canadian Football League) against the middle. Weinmeister, a Pro Football Hall of Fame defensive tackle, did time in all three pro football leagues from the late forties to the mid-fifties. Dobbs also took bigger Canadian bucks to play north of the border. Linemen, used to "$100-a-game, take it or leave it," were now demanding, and getting, salaries of $7,500-$9,000 a season. Marquee names such as Otto Graham, Steve Van Buren and Bob Waterfield were approaching the $20,000 level.

All this meant that the team owners were being drained financially. By the close of the forties, owners in both the AAFC and NFL were eager to sue for peace. It came on December 9, 1949.

In the two-league merger, orchestrated by NFL Commissioner Bert Bell, the AAFC's Baltimore Colts, Cleveland Browns, San Francisco 49ers and the Brooklyn Dodgers-New York Yankees combination (to be known as the New York Yanks) would come into the NFL for the 1950 season. Players' salaries would drop, but fan interest would pick up in the next decade – helped by an ally few in pro football realized they had at the time.

A footnote to the forties, but an important one, was the

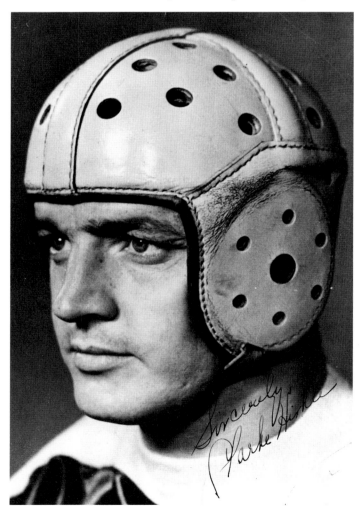

breaking of the so-called "colorline," which had kept black players out of the NFL since 1934. In 1946 both the AAFC and the NFL signed their first black players. The Los Angeles Rams, bowing to public pressure, put Kenny Washington under contract in the spring of '46, and followed that signing by coming to terms with Washington's UCLA teammate Woody Strode. The Cleveland Browns also signed Marion Motley, who had played for Paul Brown at the Great Lakes Naval Training Station during the war, in 1946; and then quickly signed Bill Willis, who had played for Brown at Ohio State. Both Motley and Willis are members of the Pro Football Hall of Fame.

Kenny Washington, whose last season at UCLA was 1939, was well past his prime, but still showed flashes of brilliance in his three-year career with the Rams. Strode, who also played his last college season in '39, played only a season with the Rams before moving on to the Canadian Football League.

Pro football's expansion was an idea whose time had come in the late forties. Public enthusiasm for the sport, increasing numbers of talented players, and the continued team leadership of such coaching greats as George Halas and Paul Brown would take pro football to new heights in the decade to come.

Pages 12-13: *The Cleveland Browns revel in their 1948 AAFC Championship victory over the Buffalo Bills, 49-7. Paul Brown (in hat) is in the middle of his players shaking hands with victory-cigar smoker, team owner Arthur "Mickey" McBride.*

Opposite: *Clarke Hinkle, Bucknell University alumnus, spoke for all two-way, sixty-minute NFL players of his era when his answer to "How long did you play?" was "Twenty years – ten on defense and ten on offense." Hinkle was a feared fullback/linebacker for the Green Bay Packers from 1932 to 1941, and was regarded by many as the game's fiercest competitor. His mano a mano confrontations with Bronko Nagurski are legendary. Hinkle retired as the NFL's all-time leading rusher, and remained so until Steve Van Buren surpassed his mark a decade later.*

Above: *As they would do often in the forties, the Chicago Bears celebrate an NFL title – this one over the Giants in 1946. Celebrants (left to right) are Sid Luckman, George McAfee, and Ray "Scooter" McLean.*

DECADE STANDINGS – 1940s NFL

Team	W-L-T	Percentage
Chicago Bears[1]	81-26-3	.750
Washington Redskins[2]	65-41-4	.609
Green Bay Packers[3]	62-44-4	.582
Philadelphia Eagles[4]	58-47-5	.550
New York Giants	55-47-8	.536
Cleveland/Los Angeles Rams[5]	50-45-5	.525
Chicago Cardinals[6]	41-65-4	.391
Pittsburgh Steelers	40-64-6	.391
Brooklyn Dodgers/Tigers	20-33-0	.377
Detroit Lions	35-71-4	.336
Boston Yanks	14-38-3	.269
New York Bulldogs	1-10-1	.091

[1]won NFL titles in 1940, 1941, 1943 and 1946.
[2]won NFL title in 1942.
[3]won NFL title in 1944.
[4]won NFL titles in 1948 and 1949.
[5]won NFL title in 1945.
[6]won NFL title in 1947.

DECADE STANDINGS – 1940s ALL-AMERICA FOOTBALL CONFERENCE

Team	W-L-T	Percentage
Cleveland Browns[1]	47-4-3	.898
San Francisco 49ers	38-14-2	.722
New York Yankees	35-17-2	.667
Los Angeles Dons	25-27-2	.481
Buffalo Bisons/Bills	23-26-5	.472
Baltimore Colts	10-29-1	.263
Chicago Rockets/Hornets	11-40-3	.231
Brooklyn Dodgers	8-32-2	.200
Miami Seahawks	3-11-0	.154

[1]won AAFC titles in 1946, 1947, 1948 and 1949.

"FIRST, LET 'EM GET A FOOTBALL"
The All-America Football Conference

Left: *The AAFC got a football –
coaches and players, too. Ace Parker
(7), a Hall of Famer, was one of
many NFL veterans who took bigger
AAFC bucks and jumped to the new
league with the New York Yankees.
The versatile Parker also played
major league baseball and was one of
the few players to hit a home run in
his first at-bat. In the NFL, Parker
raised the level of play of the
Brooklyn Dodgers to where they could
compete with, and defeat on occasion,
the New York Football Giants.
Coming out of Duke as an All-
America in 1937, Parker was a true
triple-threat. He could run, pass and
kick. His given name was Clarence.*

Opposite above: *Hardy Brown
(center, dark jersey) of the Chicago
Rockets, shown laying the lumber to a
hapless runner, usually got his man –
with a well-placed shoulder pad under
the chin, instead of a more
conventional tackle. The 190-pound
Brown, whose meanness some say
could be traced back to his childhood
in an orphanage, was nicknamed
"Thumper." Once when Bob
Waterfield of the Rams stepped off a
curb in downtown Los Angeles and
was knocked down by a Volkswagen,
he got up, dusted himself off, and
deadpanned, "Hardy Brown's back
in town." Brown's career peaked with
the 49ers in the fifties. He played in
the AAFC, the NFL and the AFL.*

Opposite below: *Like Parker,
Bruiser Kinard was an ex-NFL
Brooklyn Dodger who played in the
AAFC after the war. Kinard (nearly
no one knew his first name was
Frank) was a relentless two-way
tackle whose skills got him elected to
the Pro Football Hall of Fame in
Canton, Ohio. From Mississippi and
an All-America there, Kinard later
became an athletic director at Ole
Miss. He played at 6' 1", 218 pounds.*

The Original All-America Football Conference – 1946		
Team	Coach	Colors
Brooklyn Dodgers	Dr. Mal Stevens	Dodger blue and white
Buffalo Bisons	Lowell "Red" Dawson	Silver and royal blue
Chicago Rockets	Dick Hanley	Scarlet and white
Cleveland Browns	Paul Brown	Seal brown, orange and white
Los Angeles Dons	Dud DeGroot	Red, white and blue
Miami Seahawks	Jack Meagher	Orange and white
New York Yankees	Ray "Red" Flaherty	Silver and navy blue
San Francisco 49ers	Buck Shaw	Cardinal and silver

Opposite: *Paul Brown (left) of the Cleveland Browns, the most innovative pro coach of all time, draws diagrams in the snow in 1946 as Browns Bill Willis, one of the first blacks to play modern-day pro football, Edgar "Special Delivery" Jones, and assistant Fritz Heisler observe the strategy.*

Above: *Glenn Dobbs, the backfield ace of the AAFC Brooklyn Dodgers in 1946, frolics with entrants of a Miami Beach "Swim for Health" contest while in town to play a December game against the one-year Miami Seahawks. Poor crowds, caused by rainy weather and a losing team, forced the Seahawks to fold after the season. The franchise became the Baltimore Colts in 1947.*

Right: *Otto Graham, who would play in a championship game in each of his 10 seasons as a pro, gets a pat on the back from Coach Brown after a Browns victory in one such game. Graham, Brown, and the Browns won every AAFC Championship Game ever played – 1946-49.*

TOO GOOD, TOO SOON
The Cleveland Browns

Left above: *Dante Lavelli, a great high school hurdler who played only freshman football at Ohio State before going off to war, was a mainstay with the Cleveland Browns. He was elected to the Pro Football Hall of Fame after his career. With his large, strong hands, Lavelli was nicknamed "Gluefingers." He teamed with opposite end Mac Speedie to give Otto Graham a pair of sure-handed and reliable targets.*

Left below: *Lou "the Toe" Groza – another Browns Hall of Famer and one who, too, played only freshman ball at Ohio State – was an early kicking specialist, and then some. He played offensive tackle well enough to be named All-Pro regardless of his kicking skills. Here he practices with holder Don Greenwood. Groza's career spanned 1946-67. He scored 259 points in the AAFC and 1349 in the NFL. Note tape on the ground behind Groza's left foot. He used a 36-inch strip – later attached to a tee – to get himself lined up to kick.*

Opposite above: *By 1948 the Browns were so far ahead of the rest of the AAFC – and the NFL as it would later turn out – that they breezed through the 14-game regular season schedule undefeated and seldom challenged. As noted earlier, they thrashed the Bills in the title game, 49-7.*

Opposite below: *The scene was getting too familiar, only the Browns' players in the photos were changing. This picture of the 1949 Browns after their championship victory over the San Francisco 49ers, 21-7, shows George Young (52), Groza (behind Young), Special Delivery Jones (with Paul Brown on his shoulders), Lou Saban (20), and Cliff Lewis (over Saban's shoulder). A similar photo would be taken the next year, with the Browns in the NFL.*

BREAKING THE LINE
The First Blacks in Modern Pro Football

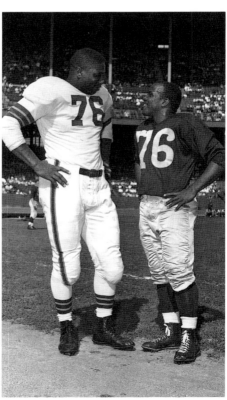

Above: *Sprinter Buddy Young (76) of Illinois was one of the first blacks to play modern-day pro football. He came to the New York Yankees of the AAFC in 1947. A personable player, he inspired the comment, "If you don't like Buddy Young, you don't like people."*

Right: *Marion Motley (left) may have shared a number with Young, but his size (6' 1", 238 lbs.) dwarfs Young's (5' 5", 170 lbs.). Motley and Bill Willis, another of Paul Brown's Ohio State proteges, were the first two black players signed by the AAFC, in 1946.*

Opposite: *Kenny Washington (13), a 1939 All-America and UCLA teammate of Jackie Robinson, was actually the first black player to sign a modern-day pro football contract. The L.A. Rams signed the hometown legend, and Woody Strode, in 1946.*

Opposite: *Paul "Tank" Younger was not only an early black in the NFL, he was the first player from an historically-black college – Grambling – to play in the NFL when he debuted with the Los Angeles Rams in 1949. The 235-pounder was equally good as a fullback and linebacker. He's wearing a Rams helmet that shows the NFL's first-ever helmet logo. Artist/halfback Fred Gehrke of the Rams handpainted each helmet with the now-famous Rams horns. While other players enjoyed Mondays off, Gehrke would touch up the battle-scarred headgear.*

Right: *Otto Graham of the Cleveland Browns (left) had the strong back and legs of Marion Motley to protect him much of his career. Motley and Bill Willis, as noted, signed in the summer of '46 to integrate the AAFC.*

Below: *Paul Brown (middle) further integrated his Browns by signing prolific punter Horace Gillom in 1947. Gillom, like Lin Houston (right), who "blocked Marion Motley into the Hall of Fame," played for Brown at fabled Washington High in Massillon, Ohio, in the thirties.*

EARLY EINSTEINS
Early Pro Coaching Greats

Opposite: *Earle "Greasy" Neale (left) with his "franchise," Steve Van Buren, was quick to follow George Halas's lead to the T-formation and transform the Philadelphia Eagles from tailender to contender. From 1944 to 1949, Neale compiled a 48-16-3 record with two NFL Championships.*

Right: *Earl "Curly" Lambeau, a hometown hero at Green Bay's East High, later coached the Packers for 29 years. Here he's flanked by Hall of Famer Don Hutson (14) and passing ace Irv Comp (51).*

Below: *Lambeau whoops it up after he and the boys defeated the Giants, 14-7, for the 1944 NFL title. Lambeau would later be fired by the Packers, and finish his NFL career coaching the Chicago Cardinals and Washington Redskins. For many years, however, Lambeau's 220 NFL wins were second only to George Halas's 325. Today, Lambeau still trails only Halas, Don Shula and Tom Landry in NFL regular season coaching victories.*

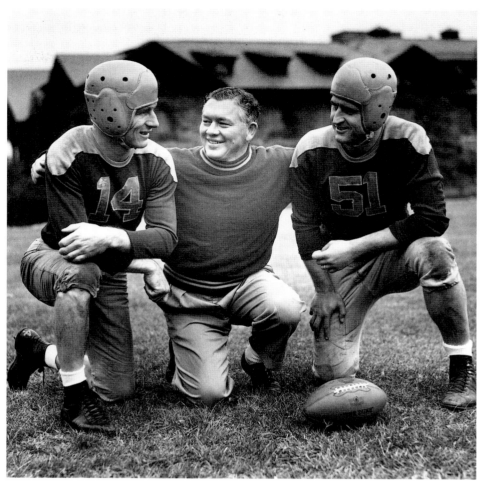

Left: *Steve Owen (striped baseball pants) inspects his squad with (left to right) Jack Mara and his father, Tim. Owen, who developed the "umbrella" defense, was regarded as a defensive genius. He coached the New York Giants for 23 seasons (1931-53) with no contract – just a handshake.*

Below: *"Stout Steve," as Owen was called, is flanked by a pair of ex-All-America tackles – Jim White (77) of Notre Dame and DeWitt "Tex" Coulter (79) of Army. Once, after losing 63-7 to the Steelers, Owen said, "Gee, I'm glad I'm a defensive genius – no telling what the score could have been."*

Right: *Chicago Bears George Halas (left) and his quarterback Sid Luckman (right) discuss some football nuances with famed columnist Walter Winchell during the forties.*

Below: *Halas (left) looks over play diagrams – while wearing four-buckle arctic boots – with (left to right) quarterbacks Young Bussey, who would lose his life in WW II, and Bob Snyder, and ends Ken Kavanaugh and Dick Plasman, in 1941. Plasman is the answer to the trivia question: Who was the last NFL player to not wear a helmet? Still the NFL's winningest head coach, Halas coached his Bears for 40 years.*

RE-TOOLING
Making Quarterbacks from Tailbacks

Roster Limits – NFL, 1943-1992; AFL, 1960-69	
Years	No. of Players
1946-49	33
1950-54	32
1955-59	33
1960-64	38
1960-64 (AFL)	35
1965-70	40
1965-69 (AFL)	38
1971-75	43
1976-92	45

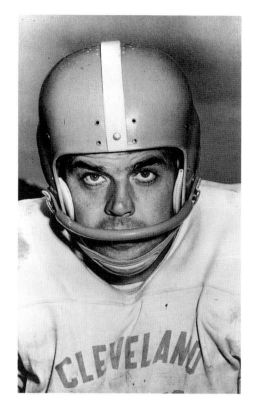

Opposite: *Two great single-wing tailbacks chose different paths in the NFL. "Ol' 98," Tom Harmon, Michigan's Heisman Trophy winner, became a halfback; Bob Waterfield (7) became a Hall of Fame T-formation quarterback, but one who could still run, pass and kick. Both Harmon and Waterfield played with the L.A. Rams. Both Harmon and Waterfield married movie actresses – Harmon, Elyse Knox; Waterfield, Jane Russell.*

Above: *Otto Graham illustrated the versatility required of a single-winger. He made the move to T-quarterback from tailback, and led the Cleveland Browns for a glorious decade. He even played pro basketball, and was an accomplished musician. Graham is wearing a single-bar facemask patented by his coach, Paul Brown.*

Right: *Sid Luckman (42) never played a down of T-formation football at Columbia, yet George Halas acquired him for the Chicago Bears on his potential as a T-quarterback in 1939. Luckman, being rushed here by the Giants' Al Blozis (32) – an NCAA shotput champion who was killed in WW II – threw for 7 touchdowns in this November 14, 1943 game. It was an NFL single-game record and has only been tied, never broken.*

UNDER A CLOUD
The '46 NFL Championship Tainted with Gambling Rumors

Opposite above: *Neither rumors nor a hard-fought game keep the Chicago Bears from rejoicing in victory after winning the 1946 NFL Championship. Sid Luckman (42, center) joins fellow players, and even the Bears' mascot, in the traditional locker room post-game whoopla.*

Opposite below: *Rumors circulated that the 1946 NFL championship game was going to be "fixed." Suspected were New York Giants halfbacks Frankie Filchock (40, shown with coach Steve Owen during the game) and Merle Hapes. The word on the street was they had been offered bribes to make sure the Giants lost to the Bears. Filchock denied the rumors and played; Hapes was prevented from dressing for the game. Filchock "played his heart out" in a losing cause, throwing two touchdown passes – despite receiving a broken nose in the early going – to tie the game at 14-14. The Bears were just too much and prevailed eventually, 24-14. Later, Hapes and Filchock would be banned from the NFL, not because they took bribes, but because they failed to report the bribe offers to the proper authorities. Filchock would go on to play in the Canadian Football League, and later become the Denver Broncos' first head coach when the AFL began in 1960.*

Right above: *Newly-elected NFL commissioner Bert Bell (left) is shown with Hapes, who along with Filchock, was suspended immediately after a jury found reputed gambler Alvin J. Paris guilty of the attempted bribes.*

Right below: *Alvin Paris is shown leaving the New York district attorney's office after being indicted on two counts of attempted bribery. Paris was found guilty in a January 1947 trial. It wasn't known at the time, but other gamblers were already deeply involved in giving bribes to New York City area college basketball players to "shave" points in games. Perhaps because of the Paris attempt, the NFL acted to have league security personnel check thoroughly into even a hint of impropriety. To date, the NFL has escaped the embarrassment other major sports have had to endure.*

HIGH FLYING CARDINALS
The Cardinals' Last NFL Championship

Left: *Charley Trippi (62), out of the University of Georgia, supplied much of the lightning to the Chicago Cardinals' attack as they won the franchise's last NFL Championship in 1947. Trippi was just one of many from the Pennsylvania anthracite coal region (Pittston) to head south to play college football. The future Hall of Famer ran from scrimmage, returned punts and kickoffs, passed, punted, played defense, and even socked cross-town "bad boy" Ed Sprinkle of the Bears in the nose. Not many NFL players ever "got" Sprinkle.*

Below: *Dapper Jimmy Conzelman, after leading the Providence (Rhode Island) Steam Roller to an NFL title in 1928, took the Cardinals to the '47 championship. Although the franchise moved to St. Louis and on to Phoenix, it has never won another NFL title.*

Opposite above: *To win in '47, the Cards had to get past Philadelphia. Here Trippi drags Joe Muha of the Eagles, while Plato Andros (68) and Vic Sears (79) arrive on the scene.*

Opposite below: *Paul Christman, Cardinals quarterback (44, right side of photo) has launched a pass that will be caught by Billy Dewell (41, dark jersey). The Cardinals won, 28-21, as Trippi and Elmer Angsman each had two long scoring runs.*

SOARING WITH EAGLES
Philadelphia Eagles Championship Teams

Left: *One-eyed wonder Tommy Thompson (left, with Philadelphia Eagles general manager Harry Thayer and would-be Eagle Freddy Myers) provided the 1948 and 1949 championship teams with great passing. He and Myers are about to be mustered out of the service in time for the 1945 season. Thompson got himself and teammates out of many a hot August practice by suggesting to coach Greasy Neale that it was a "good afternoon for a quick nine holes." Golfing never interfered with winning, though.*

Below: *The 1948 Eagles won the NFL Championship, 7-0, in a rematch with the Chicago Cardinals. The '49 Eagles defeated the Los Angeles Rams, 14-0, for the title. It was the only time a team has won two consecutive titles by shutouts.*

Opposite: *The Eagles' Steve Van Buren was simply the best runner of his era – 1944-51.*

Opposite above: *Before the Eagles could take care of the Cardinals to take the 1948 NFL Championship, they had to take care of business – like helping to remove the Shibe Park tarpaulin.*

Opposite below: *Van Buren (15) plows for yardage in the '48 title game.*

Above: *Van Buren (foreground) tumbled into the end zone for the game's only touchdown – a five-yard, off-tackle smash – in the fourth quarter. It snowed five additional inches during the game, cutting the crowd to 28,664, and lowering the Eagles' winning share to $1,540.84 per man.*

Right: *After the game, Neale (with rumpled fedora) and Van Buren (15) hold the prized game ball. Neale, who coached Washington & Jefferson to the 1922 Rose Bowl, also played major league baseball. Neale's coaching career ended in 1950 when he tangled with club president Jim Clark after a 7-3 loss to the Giants when Clark, before team and press, said, "You gotta get more than a field goal to win in the NFL, Greasy."*

TWILIGHT OF THE GODS
Hall of Famers Ending their Careers

Opposite: *Dan Fortmann (17, shown during a 1941 game), taken by the Chicago Bears on the final round of the 1936 draft because George Halas thought his name "sounded like a football player's," became a practicing physician while still playing. A skilled surgeon who would become the Rams' team physician, Fortmann – 30 years ahead of his time – took care to add protective wraps to the hands that were so necessary to his livelihood. Fortmann was a starting guard in the NFL six months before he could cast a vote. Assistant Paddy Driscoll (holding microphone) is talking to another Bears assistant in the pressbox. Fortmann and Driscoll are Hall of Famers.*

Above: *The Packers' Clarke Hinkle (30) runs the ball during Green Bay's winning effort in the 1945 NFL Championship game vs. the Giants. Like many Hall of Famers, Hinkle ended his pro career in the forties.*

Right: *Mel Hein earned the nickname "Old Indestructible" and a niche in the Hall of Fame with the quality (NFL Most Valuable Player of 1938) and length (15 seasons) of his New York Giants career.*

Left: *Tuffy Leemans (white No. 4 on dark jersey) is dropped unceremoniously on the infield dirt of Pittsburgh's Forbes Field in this 1940 New York Giants-Steelers game. Making the stop is guard Jack Sanders (55). NFL folklore has it that Leemans, a virtual unknown, was discovered by the Giants' Wellington Mara. Young Mara was instrumental in having his father's team draft Leemans on the second round – hardly where you'd take a "sleeper" – but the part about Tuffy being an unknown is suspect. He was an honorable mention All-America at George Washington University and played in the 1936 Chicago College All-Star game – then a very big deal. He went on to lead the NFL in rushing (830 yards) as a rookie. Leemans was a mainstay in the Giants' backfield for eight seasons.*

In addition to Fortmann, Hein, Hinkle and Leemans, the following members of the Pro Football Hall of Fame ended their careers in the forties: Glen "Turk" Edwards, stellar tackle with the Boston-Washington Redskins; Arnie Herber, the main man in Curly Lambeau's Green Bay passing attack; Bill Hewitt, who during his early Chicago Bears and Philadelphia Eagles career never wore a helmet – and forced the league to make helmets mandatory when he played a final season in 1943; Don Hutson, the Packers' immortal end, who could star in today's game just as he did in the 1930s and '40s; Bruiser Kinard, a true southern gentleman – except on the gridiron; Wayne Millner, whose receiving statistics don't look like much, but whose blocking paved the way for Cliff Battles to go into the Hall of Fame; George Musso, giant Bears tackle, who played against presidents Ronald Reagan in college and Gerald R. Ford in the College All-Star game; the incomparable Bronko Nagurski; Ace Parker, about the only thing the Brooklyn Dodgers had in the backfield for years; Ken Strong, perhaps the first NFL player to be kept on a roster as a kicking specialist, but a terrific runner in his early years; and Joe Stydahar, Fortmann's Bears linemate, who once remarked to a Rams team he was coaching, "No wonder you guys are down 21 points at halftime – you all have all your teeth."

DECADE HIGHLIGHTS

Left: *Don Hutson, with Charley Brock holding, added to his point total by kicking field goals and PATs – he also scored 105 touchdowns. The Green Bay Packers' Hall of Famer led the NFL in scoring in five of his 11 years – consecutively from 1940 to 1944.*

Below: *Ken Strong played long (1929-47) and well in the NFL. He had tours of duty with the New York Giants and Staten Island Stapletons.*

Opposite: *This photo shows just how badly Don Hutson could burn an unfortunate defender. Getting "toasted" in the 1944 NFL title game – won by the Packers, 14-7 – is the Giants' Howie Livingston (24).*

DECADE LEADERS, 1940s – NFL

PASSING
Yardage: Sammy Baugh	17,002
Completion Percentage: Sammy Baugh	58.7%
Touchdowns: Sammy Baugh	149

RUSHING
Yardage: Steve Van Buren	4,904
Per Carry Average: Steve Van Buren	4.8 yards
Touchdowns: Steve Van Buren	59

RECEIVING
Receptions: Don Hutson	329
Yardage: Don Hutson	5,089 yards
Per Catch Average: Ken Kavanaugh	22.7 yards
Touchdowns: Don Hutson	63
SCORING: Don Hutson	589 points
PUNT RETURN AVERAGE: Ernie Steele	16.0 yards
KICKOFF RET. AVE.: Steve Van Buren	27.0 yards
FIELD GOALS: Ted Fritsch	33
PUNTING AVERAGE: Sammy Baugh	45.5 yards
INTERCEPTIONS: Irv Comp	33

DECADE LEADERS, 1940s – AAFC★

PASSING
Yardage: Otto Graham	10,085
Completion Percentage: Otto Graham	55.8%
Touchdowns: Frankie Albert	88

RUSHING
Yardage: Marion Motley	3,024
Per Carry Average: Marion Motley	6.2 yards
Touchdowns: Spec Sanders	33

RECEIVING
Receptions: Mac Speedie	211
Yardage: Mac Speedie	3,554 yards
Per Catch Average: Dante Lavelli	18.2 yards
Touchdowns: Alyn Beals	46
SCORING: Alyn Beals	278 points
PUNT RETURN AVERAGE: Spec Sanders	15.25 yards
KICKOFF RET. AVE.: Chet Mutryn	27.66 yards
FIELD GOALS: Lou Groza	30
PUNTING AVERAGE: Glenn Dobbs	46.4 yards
INTERCEPTIONS: Cliff Lewis	24

★*AAFC existed only from 1946-49.*

Left and below: *Bullet Bill Dudley had limited natural ability, but no one wanted to win more than did this 5' 10", 176-pounder. In his Hall of Fame career, he played three seasons in each of three cities – Pittsburgh, Detroit and Washington. Dudley had a knack for setting up and following his blockers. In the action shot, Dudley (with the ball) is on his way to a 95-yard touchdown on a punt return during a 1942 charity game between the NFL All-Stars and the champion Washington Redskins. Dudley was not only intelligent, but versatile. In 1946 he led the NFL in rushing – an offensive category; in interceptions – a defensive category; and in punt returns – a special teams category. He won the official NFL MVP Award, and it's safe to say no one will ever lead the league in categories representing the three platoons of the game in the same season.*

Opposite above: *Commissioner Bert Bell, selected to the post in 1946 after being a coach and team owner, presides at a draft meeting. It was Bell who conceived the draft in 1935.*

Opposite below: *Bert Bell (center) and Washington Redskins owner George Preston Marshall (right) called at the White House in 1947 to present Harry S Truman with a gold NFL season pass.*

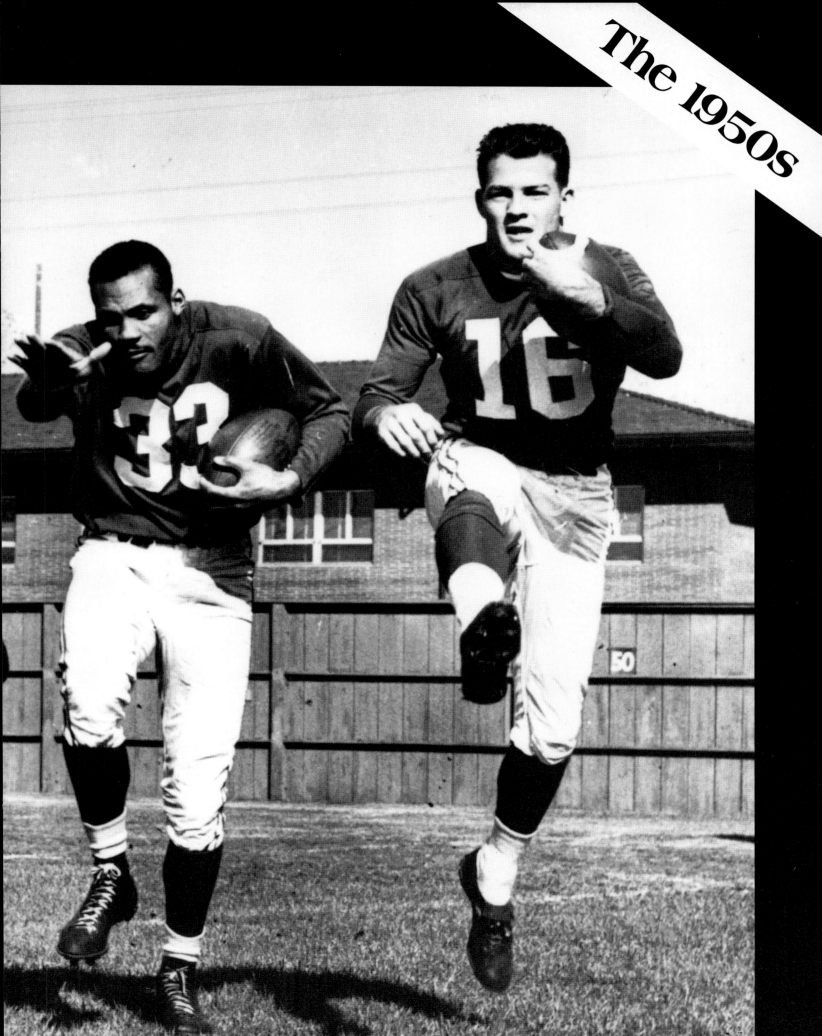

The post-war boom of the late 1940s continued into the fifties, touching all phases of daily life in America. For the NFL, the fifties represented unprecedented growth. Attendance at games jumped to an average of 43,617 per game by the end of the decade – up from 8,211 in the early 1930s, when the league first kept viable attendance figures and was basically a collection of town teams.

The NFL – the only pro football league in the nation for the decade – had settled into a 12-team confederation of two six-team divisions. The fifties are often referred to as "the Golden Age of (fill in the blank)." Certainly, the golden age could be applied to the NFL.

Peace with the AAFC had stabilized player salaries. Yet the pay was still high enough that an All-America guard from Texas Christian or an All-Coast fullback from UCLA would want to play with the New York Giants or Washington Redskins. Roster limits were relatively low, the pay was relatively high, and the hours could compare favorably with those of bankers. Competition for jobs being what it was, simply stated – if you played in the NFL in the 1950s, you were a helluva football player. By way of illustration, nearly half of the players in the Pro Football Hall of Fame played all or parts of their NFL careers in the fifties.

The national scope of pro football brought about other changes. Train travel was used less and less. Plane travel was used more and more. With teams on both coasts, it was necessary to take to the air. No longer would the Giants take a boat along the Atlantic coast to play the Redskins, as they once did. The league was too big for that.

Television, with its probing red light and gray eye, was on the scene. The first televised NFL game had occurred in 1939 – about a decade earlier than most people would guess. But like the production of the plastic suspension helmet and civilian automobiles, the development of TV was inhibited by the war.

The Los Angeles Rams were the first team to experiment with televising all their games – home and away. While providing a great service to the viewing public, it didn't help the Rams' treasury. People simply stopped going and paying for what they could stay at home and see free. Something needed to be done as other teams – most notably the Redskins – made their own TV deals. That something was a ruling by Commissioner Bert Bell. The NFL would "black out" home games and televise only away games. This proved a very wise move. People had to, once again, pay to see their hometown favorites at the stadium, but could see their local heroes on TV playing road games. The advantage was twofold. It increased stadium attendance and created vastly more attention and interest with the away games being beamed back to the local area. Not only that, but areas with no "home team" were also getting weekly telecasts of NFL football. Fans throughout the nation saw pro football in the comfort of their living rooms and were quickly taken in by the skill, speed, strength and even the ruthless determination of these modern day gladiators.

For the first time, in 1951, the NFL championship game was televised coast-to-coast. It cost the DuMont Network $75,000 to bring the Rams' 24-17 defeat of the Browns into the nation's living rooms.

Commissioner Bell was quick to see that TV could be a strong friend, or a formidable foe, if not properly

NFL Per-Game Offensive Statistics: 1953-57 vs. 1990-91		
	1953-57	1990-91
First Downs	17.10	17.76
Points	20.88	19.55
Touchdowns	2.64	2.21
TD-Rushing	1.15	0.82
TD-Passing	1.26	1.21
TD-Runbacks	0.22	0.18
PATs	2.50	2.13
Safeties	0.03	0.02
Field Goals	0.80	1.36

DECADE STANDINGS – 1950s

Team	W-L-T	Percentage
Cleveland Browns[1]	88-33-2	.742
New York Giants[2]	74-41-3	.646
Chicago Bears	70-48-2	.592
Detroit Lions[3]	68-48-4	.583
Los Angeles Rams[4]	68-49-3	.579
San Francisco 49ers	63-54-3	.538
Pittsburgh Steelers	54-63-3	.463
Philadelphia Eagles	51-64-5	.446
Baltimore Colts[5]	42-53-1	.442
Washington Redskins	47-70-3	.404
New York Yanks	8-14-2	.363
Green Bay Packers	39-79-2	.333
Chicago Cardinals	33-84-3	.288
Dallas Texans	1-11-0	.083

[1] won NFL titles in 1950, 1954 and 1955.
[2] won NFL title in 1956.
[3] won NFL titles in 1952, 1953 and 1957.
[4] won NFL title in 1951.
[5] won NFL titles in 1958 and 1959.

Pages 48-49: *The backfield of the 1956 East Pro Bowl squad – Eddie LeBaron, Johnny Olszewski, Ollie Matson and Frank Gifford – pose in practice.*

Opposite above: *Y. A. Tittle (with football), as the San Francisco 49ers' quarterback in 1956, bolts into the end zone despite the efforts of 280-pound Green Bay Packers tackle Jerry Helluin.*

Opposite below: *Frank Gifford (left) and Charlie Conerly are two happy New York Giants. They have just defeated the Browns for the 1959 Eastern Division title. While the Giants would win the East many times from 1956 to 1963, they would win the NFL Championship only once – 1956.*

regulated. While the courts upheld the blackout rule, the NFL had a harder time trying to negotiate a "single network" TV package. Because of this, each team made its own deal. As might be expected, a contending team like the Giants in New York could gain more TV dollars than a tailender like the Packers in Green Bay, Wisconsin.

Some teams were able to extract as much as $100,000 a year for the rights to their broadcasts, but this was the exception rather than the rule. It would not be until the early 1960s that the league would have a "collective" television agreement, one that would pay each team equally – as much as $300,000 a season – regardless of whether it was Green Bay, Los Angeles, Pittsburgh or New York. The figures would go up, dramatically, from there.

Fans could stay home and see future Hall of Famers on their 10-inch screens, but many opted to go to the stadium and see the twisting runs of Hugh McElhenny and Lenny Moore, the spiralling passes of Norm Van Brocklin and Y.A. Tittle, the head-on collisions of Hardy Brown and Joe Schmidt. It was a heady decade for the NFL, and nothing proved this more than the 1958 sudden death Championship Game between the Giants and the Colts. It was this game, more than any other, that tied the knot between the fan, the NFL and TV. The NFL was riding a crest. Things were so good that in 1959 a group of young visionaries decided that they should hang-ten on the surfboard of popularity as it rode pro football's version of "the perfect wave" – and the AFL hit the beach running.

AIRMAIL SPECIAL DELIVERY
Great Passers

Left: *Bobby Layne was a true Texas legend, on and off the field. The blond bomber retired in 1962 with every significant NFL passing record. Layne was the master, and the first and best practitioner, of the two-minute drill. Whether Layne was playing for the Chicago Bears, New York Bulldogs, Detroit Lions – where he defined the sport in the fifties – or Pittsburgh Steelers, the only protection he wore was a helmet and skimpy shoulder pads. No facemask, no rib pads, no hip pads, no thigh pads, no knee pads. Off the field, teammate Harley Sewell captured the quintessential Layne with this one-liner: "We went out Thursday night for a tube of toothpaste, and didn't get home until Saturday." Columnist Jim Murray, at the time of Layne's death shortly before he turned 60, wrote, "for Bobby, life was all fast Layne."*

Opposite above: *Layne exhibited less than textbook form in anything he did. "All he could do was beat you," it was said. Here he scores in the Lions' 1952 NFL Championship victory.*

Opposite below: *The Los Angeles Rams' Norm Van Brocklin (11, far left) was also a Hall of Fame quarterback. Here he passes for a 10-yard gain in the 1955 NFL title game vs. the Browns.*

Comparison of Pro Football Hall of Fame Quarterbacks' Career Passing Statistics: 1950s vs. More Recent

1950s Player	Attempts	Completions	%	Yards	TDs	Interceptions
Sammy Baugh	2,995	1,693	56.5	21,886	187	203
George Blanda	4,007	1,911	47.7	26,920	236	277
Otto Graham	2,626	1,464	55.8	23,584	174	135
Bobby Layne	3,700	1,814	49.0	26,768	196	243
Y.A. Tittle	4,395	2,427	55.2	33,070	242	248
Norm Van Brocklin	2,895	1,553	53.6	23,611	173	178
Bob Waterfield	1,617	814	50.3	11,849	97	128
Recent Players						
Len Dawson	3,741	2,136	57.1	28,711	239	183
Sonny Jurgensen	4,262	2,433	57.1	32,224	255	189
Bart Starr	3,149	1,808	57.7	24,718	152	138
Johnny Unitas	5,186	2,830	54.6	40,239	290	253
Bob Griese	3,429	1,926	56.2	25,092	192	172
Joe Namath	3,762	1,886	50.1	27,663	173	220
Roger Staubach	2,958	1,685	57.0	22,700	153	109
Fran Tarkenton	6,467	3,686	57.0	47,003	342	266

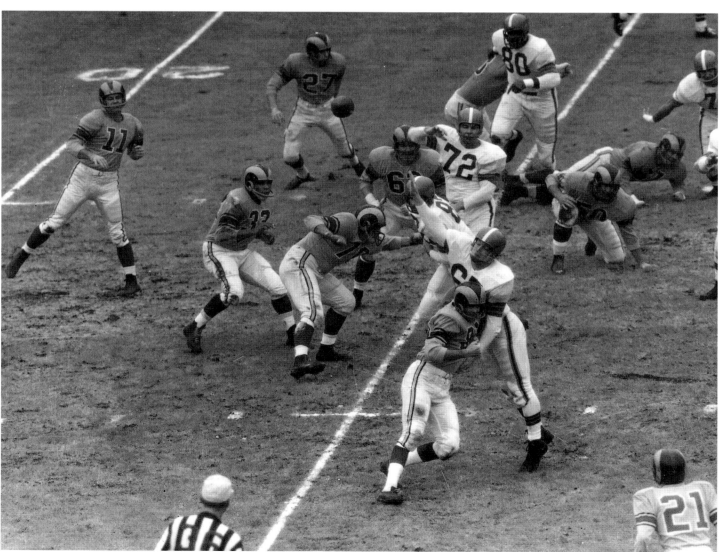

Left: *After winning another championship in 1954, Otto Graham of the Cleveland Browns kisses his helmet. Having once had his face crunched in, he is probably thankful for the single-bar facemask that his coach, Paul Brown, invented.*

Below: *New York Giants quarterback Charlie Conerly (42), like many QBs of his time, could run as well as throw. In this game against the Browns, he is attempting to evade future Hall of Famer Bill Willis (60). Conerly was once featured in print ads as the Marlboro man. Late in his career, he was part of a unique quarterback situation. Although Chuckin' Charlie was the first-string QB, Don Heinrich would start and probe the opposing defenses while Conerly observed from the sidelines. Conerly would usually play more than three quarters. Probably because Conerly did not have a large ego, the system worked well. The consummate team player, Conerly also accepted a backup role with no muttering when the Giants obtained Y. A. Tittle in 1961.*

Opposite: *Johnny Lujack (32), a Heisman Trophy winner at Notre Dame in 1947, had a brief (1948-51) but brilliant career with the Chicago Bears. A great passer, he was also outstanding on defense when a shoulder injury limited his passing.*

THE GOOD HANDS PEOPLE
Receivers

Opposite: *Elroy "Crazylegs" Hirsch (40) has eluded Browns defensive back Cliff Lewis to take a pass as Hirsch's Los Angeles Rams defeated Cleveland for the 1951 NFL championship, 24-17. With Hirsch, Tom Fears and Bob Boyd catching, and Bob Waterfield and Norm Van Brocklin throwing, the Rams set offensive records that still stand four decades later. Hirsch, a great runner in college (Wisconsin and Michigan), was one of the first to convert to flanker and become almost exclusively a receiver.*

Left above: *Tom Fears caught 84 passes in 1950, a record unbroken for 10 years. Fears wore Adidas soccer shoes 40 years before today's sneaker wars. The L.A. Rams' end said, "They just felt better than football shoes. I didn't have a 'deal' with them."*

Left below: *Raymond Berry got more out of limited natural ability than any receiver who ever played the game. He reduced pass catching to a science. He and Baltimore Colts teammate Johnny Unitas worked the sideline pattern like no one before or since. In 13 seasons, Berry caught 631 passes (an NFL record at the time) for 9,275 yards. He later took the New England Patriots to the Super Bowl as head coach.*

Page 58: *Even while he was an effective runner, Frank Gifford (16) was an ace receiver for the New York Giants. His 367 receptions are still second-best in team history.*

Page 59: *Elroy Hirsch catches a pass from Norm Van Brocklin in this 1954 Rams win over the Giants.*

RIGHT IN YOUR LIVING ROOM
TV Comes to the NFL

A Comparison of 1950s NFL Teams' Home and Away Records

Cleveland Browns	Home 45-15	Away 43-15-2
New York Giants	Home 38-19-3	Away 38-22
Chicago Bears	Home 39-20-1	Away 31-28-1
Detroit Lions	Home 38-22-2	Away 30-27-2
Los Angeles Rams	Home 40-18-1	Away 28-31-2
San Francisco 49ers	Home 38-22	Away 25-32-3
Pittsburgh Steelers	Home 30-28-2	Away 24-35-1
Philadelphia Eagles	Home 35-24-1	Away 16-40-4
Baltimore Colts	Home 26-21-1	Away 16-32
Washington Redskins	Home 26-32-2	Away 21-38-1
New York Yanks	Home 5-4-1	Away 3-6-1
Green Bay Packers	Home 23-36-1	Away 16-43-1
Chicago Cardinals	Home 18-38-3	Away 15-46
Dallas Texans*	Home 0-4	Away 1-7

After seven games of the 1952 season, the NFL took over the franchise and headquartered the team in Hershey, PA, from where they played only "road" games. The Texans' lone victory was a 27-23 Thanksgiving Day win over the Chicago Bears in neutral Akron, Ohio.

Opposite above: *Skip Walz became the first TV sportscaster on October 22, 1939, when he did play-by-play of the Brooklyn Dodgers-Philadelphia Eagles game for NBC. It occurred about a decade earlier than most would guess.*

Opposite below: *Early technicians worked with rather simple equipment.*

Right: *Viewers of early black-and-white TV had a hard time telling the San Francisco 49ers' red jerseys from the Deroit Lions' blue ones. No. 34 is 49er Joe Perry (with the ball).*

Below: *Forward-thinking coaches such as Hall of Famer Ray Flaherty found more than entertainment value in TV. He used it to check overhead views of game action from the sidelines.*

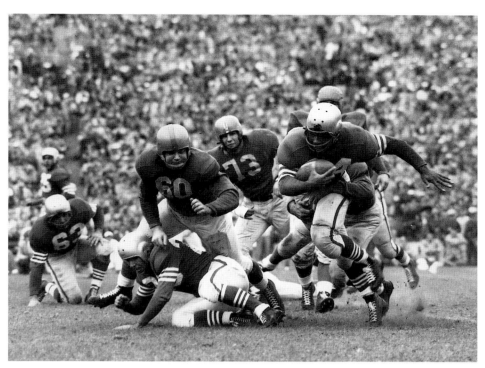

STOPPERS

Opposite: *Jack Butler, defensive back for the Pittsburgh Steelers from 1951 to 1959, played well enough to merit inclusion in the Pro Football Hall of Fame. However, he's still waiting for Canton to make its move. When a debilitating leg injury forced him to retire in '59, Butler had 52 career interceptions – behind only Hall of Famers Emlen Tunnell and Dick "Night Train" Lane. Butler was a dangerous receiver when occasionally employed on offense.*

Right: *Tackle Eugene "Big Daddy" Lipscomb was a force when motivated, but one respected Baltimore writer described him as "an in-and-outer."*

Below: *The 6' 6", 288-pound Lipscomb – a giant at the time – played only high school football before signing with the Los Angeles Rams. Here he hoists 6' 4" defensive back Don Burroughs (25) on his shoulders in an attempt to block a field goal.*

Pages 64-65: *Emlen Tunnell (45, dark jersey), the first defensive specialist to be enshrined in Canton's Pro Football Hall of Fame, is still the second-leading all-time NFL interceptor. His 79 career pass-thefts trail only Paul Krause's 81. Tunnell, who walked into the New York Giants' offices in 1948 and asked for a tryout, was also a formidable kick returner. In 1952 his 924 yards on returns was a better total than the 894 yards compiled by the NFL's leading rusher, Deacon Dan Towler. In this four-picture sequence, Tunnell, who played at Toledo and Iowa, breaks up a pass intended for Eagles halfback Ted Wegert in a 1955 Giants-Eagles game. The Giants, thanks to Tunnell and his defensive mates, crushed the Eagles, 31-7. Tunnell followed his defensive coach Vince Lombardi to Green Bay in 1959 and brought a winning spirit to a Packers team that had been 1-10-1 in 1958.*

MIDDLEMEN

Left above: *Bill George of the Chicago Bears may have been the best at his position, while Sam Huff got more media exposure than all other middle linebackers combined. After the CBS-TV special "The Violent World of Sam Huff," it was said: "If they ever make a Hollywood feature film of that [Violent World], Bill George should play the lead role, Joe Schmidt should direct, and Les Richter produce." George came to the Bears as a middle guard in 1952 from Wake Forest. He complained to veteran lineman George Connor that he "couldn't see" playing on the center's nose. Connor, a crafty five-year man at the time, told the rookie to drop a yard back and stand up. That's how middle linebacking came about. George, a Pro Bowler for much of his Bears career, followed his defensive coach George Allen to the Rams in 1965 for a final season. He was inducted into the Pro Football Hall of Fame in 1974.*

Left below: *Les Richter came to the Los Angeles Rams in an 11-man trade – that's right, Richter for a whole team. Though he played on some poor teams in his nine-year career, he stood out as a power in the middle.*

Opposite above left and right: *Sam Huff was the middle linebackers' coverboy. There are NFL insiders who will tell you that he was glamorized beyond his talent by a tailor-made Giants defense and the New York media, but there are just as many who will tell you the Giants' middleman was as good as any of his contemporaries. Huff is a member of the Hall of Fame, class of '82.*

Opposite below: *The Detroit Lions toast a 1957 playoff victory with the "real thing." Celebrants (left to right) are: Tobin Rote, head coach George Wilson, Joe Schmidt, assistant Buster Ramsey, and Tom Tracy. Schmidt, somewhat undersized at 6' 1", 218, was a keen diagnostician and a smashing hitter. A Hall of Famer, he has his supporters who claim him as "the best ever."*

BAD COMPANY?
Players With Reputations as Villains

Left: *In the 1950s, in the days when hardly anyone wore a facemask, certain NFL players had reputations as villains. They were mostly linemen and linebackers. Then there was John Henry Johnson, a fullback with the San Francisco 49ers, Detroit Lions and Pittsburgh Steelers. The chin-chilling blocker formed a close friendship with Bobby Layne because of the protection he afforded Layne in the pocket, and when turned loose, he was a steamroller with the football. In his thirties, Johnson twice ran for more than 1,000 yards in a season. Paul Brown once accused John Henry of "whacking everyone in the league." JHJ replied, "Then we're even, 'cause everyone in the league has whacked me." He once was run out of bounds by a posse of tacklers and defended himself with a sideline yard marker in the ensuing confrontation. After a long delay, JHJ was inducted into the Pro Football Hall of Fame in 1987.*

Opposite: *The name Francis J. Kilroy doesn't mean much to many, but mention Bucko Kilroy and people know exactly who you mean. He has spent a half-century in the NFL in nearly every capacity, beginning as a player with the Philadelphia Eagles in 1943. As a player, player-coach, coach, scout, personnel director, general manager and vice president, Bucko has been in the NFL ever since. Currently he is a vice president with the New England Patriots. Despite a reputation as a rowdy, Kilroy once held the NFL record for playing in 176 consecutive games. Those who sought retaliation for real or imagined Kilroy transgressions were seldom successful. Bucko left his "Kilroy was here" trademark. He was just one of a number of players thought of as overly-aggressive, if not "dirty." Others could include: Ed Sprinkle, Gil Mains, linebacker Don Paul, Jim David, Jimmy Hill, Don Joyce, Bill Pellington – and the ubiquitous Hardy Brown.*

COASTAL RIVALRY
Rams and 49ers Draw 100,000-Plus

Opposite above: *Crowds of 100,000 or more weren't uncommon at Memorial Coliseum, especially when the Los Angeles Rams were taking on the San Francisco 49ers. On November 10, 1957, a crowd of 102,368 paid its way in to see the Rams defeat the 49ers, 37-24. Both teams had explosive offensive platoons. Players' names sound like a roll call at Canton – Bob Waterfield, Norm Van Brocklin, Tom Fears and Crazylegs Hirsch for the Rams; Y. A. Tittle, Hugh McElhenny, Leo Nomellini, John Henry Johnson, Bob St. Clair and Joe Perry for the Niners.*

Opposite below: *Tank Younger (35) picks up short yardage in the 1956 Rams-49ers shootout before a solid background of paying customers. The Rams won this close encounter, 33-30.*

Left above: *In the early days of the rivalry, Joe Stydahar (arm draped over Tom Fears's shoulder) coached the Rams. Later on, it was passing-game wizard Sid Gillman.*

Left below: *For a time, the 49ers' ex-quarterback Frankie Albert served as their head coach. Here the 5' 10" Albert is dwarfed by 6' 9" Bob St. Clair (79) and 6' 2" Stan Sheriff (50).*

Pages 72-73: *One of the strategies used early in the series, which began when the 49ers of the AAFC were merged into the NFL in 1950, was the Rams' Bull Elephant backfield (left to right): Dan Towler, Dick Hoerner, Tank Younger and quarterback Bob Waterfield. The Rams deployed Towler, Hoerner and Younger – all of them 225-pound fullbacks – in the three running back positions. This countered a move by the 49ers of using light linebackers to cover fleet, small runners and receivers. When the 49ers went to bigger linebackers to stop the Bulls, the Rams would switch to their Pony Backfield, featuring Glenn Davis, Skeet Quinlan, Vitamin T. Smith, and Tommy "Cricket" Kalmanir – all 170-pounders.*

The Ten Oldest NFL Stadiums

Stadium/Year Built	Team	Capacity
1. Memorial Coliseum/1923	Los Angeles Raiders	92,488
2. Soldier Field/1926	Chicago Bears	69,946
3. Municipal Stadium/1932	Cleveland Browns	80,098
4. Mile High Stadium/1948★	Denver Broncos	76,273
5. Milwaukee County Stadium/1953	Green Bay Packers (Milwaukee)	56,051
6. Lambeau Field/1957	Green Bay Packers (Green Bay)	59,543
7. Candlestick Park/1958	San Francisco 49ers	66,455
8. RFK Memorial Stadium/1961	Washington Redskins	55,683
9. Astrodome/1965	Houston Oilers	60,052
10. Anaheim Stadium/1966	Los Angeles Rams	69,008

★Originally called Bears Stadium, home of minor league baseball team.

Contrasting the Offensive Statistics of the 1951 Rams (8-4-0) with the 1991 Redskins (14-2-0) on a Per-Game Basis (Game Average in Parenthesis)

	1951 Rams	1991 Redskins
First Downs	272 (26.7)	302 (18.9)
Rushing	114 (9.5)	107 (6.7)
Passing	130 (10.8)	179 (11.2)
Penalty	28 (2.3)	16 (1.0)
Total Yards	5,409 (450.8)	5,741 (358.8)
Rushing	2,210 (184.2)	2,049 (128.1)
Passing	3,296 (274.7)	3,692 (230.8)
Rushing Attempts	426 (35.5)	540 (33.8)
Average Gain	5.2	3.8
Passing Attempts	373 (31.1)	447 (27.9)
Completion %	50.7	58.4
Interceptions	22 (1.8)	11 (0.7)
Touchdowns	51 (4.3)	56 (3.5)
Rushing	23 (1.9)	21 (1.3)
Passing	26 (2.2)	30 (1.9)
Runback	2 (0.2)	5 (0.3)
PAT	47/51	56/56
Field Goal Attempts	24 (2.0)	43 (2.7)
Field Goals	13 (1.1)	31 (1.9)
Field Goal %	54.2	72.1
Total Points	392 (32.7)	485 (30.3)

"THE GREATEST GAME EVER PLAYED"
1958 Colts vs. Giants

1958 Team Statistics Comparison: Baltimore Colts vs. New York Giants			
	COLTS	GIANTS	Advantage
OFFENSE			
First Downs	253	191	Colts
Rushing	117	93	Colts
Passing	120	83	Colts
Total Yards	4,539	3,330	Colts
Rushing	2,127	1,725	Colts
Passing	2,412	1,725	Colts
Passing-Attempts	354	266	Colts
Completions	178	119	Colts
Percentage	50.3	44.7	Colts
Yards Per Passing Attempt	6.8	6.0	Colts
Average Gain Per Play	5.6	4.7	Colts
Percentage of Rushes	56.3	62.8	Giants
Percentage of Passes	43.7	37.2	Colts
DEFENSE			
Opponents' First Downs	188	170	Giants
By Rushing	70	83	Colts
By Passing	106	80	Giants
By Penalty	12	7	Giants
Total Yards	3,284	3,418	Colts
By Rushing	1,291	1,440	Colts
By Passing	1,993	1,978	Giants
Average Gain-Pass/Rush	4.7	4.8	Colts
Points Surrendered	203	183	Giants
Opponents' TDs	27	22	Giants
Rushing	13	8	Giants
Passing	9	11	Giants
Runbacks	5	3	Giants
Field Goals	5	12	Colts

Left: *The 1958 NFL title game has been called, and is still called, "the greatest game ever played." It awakened a nation to the excitement of NFL football at the stadium, and, more importantly to more people, on television. Coast-to-coast, people watched and their hearts and minds were won over. Perhaps the most influential figure in the mystical game was Johnny Unitas, shown with an assortment of athletic equipment he endorsed – no doubt because of his newly-won celebrity as the Baltimore Colts' winning quarterback. While it didn't come close to what Michael Jordan and Bo Jackson would do later, it was a start. Unitas, drafted out of Louisville by his hometown Steelers and quickly cut by coach Walt Kiesling, was known as the Cinderella Kid. He played sandlot ball for $6 a game with a neighborhood team, the Bloomfield Rams. The Colts, according to NFL legend, placed a 65¢ phone call to acquire him for the 1956 season, and the rest – as John Facenda said – "is well-documented history."*

Opposite above: *Johnny Unitas passes during the 1958 NFL title game. In the hard-fought contest, Unitas completed 26 of 40 passes for 349 yards and one touchdown.*

Opposite below: *Alan Ameche (with ball), a workhorse all day during the 1958 title game, is dropped by Jimmy Patton (20) and Carl Karilivacz (21) and pinned by a late-arriving Sam Huff (70).*

Opposite: *As referee Ron Gibbs (8) signals that Ameche (obscured behind Raymond Berry, 82) has suddenly ended the '58 championship game with a one-yard smash off right tackle, Unitas (19) just looks at the ground and calmly walks off the field while the rest of the world goes nearly bonkers. This, as much as anything, reveals Unitas's stoic character.*

Above: *In the locker room after the 23-17 victory (left to right), Steve Myrha, Unitas, forcing a smile for the cameras, and Ameche – with something a little more potent than Myrha's soda – finally call it a day. Unitas's passing keyed the overtime drive. Myrha's 20-yard field goal tied the game in regulation. Ameche ended it all with his sudden death TD plunge.*

Right: *In another sector of the locker room, Baltimore's head coach Weeb Ewbank (center, holding the game ball) and owner Carroll Rosenbloom (right) flash jubilant victory smiles.*

HIGH-MILEAGE PERFORMANCE
Running Backs

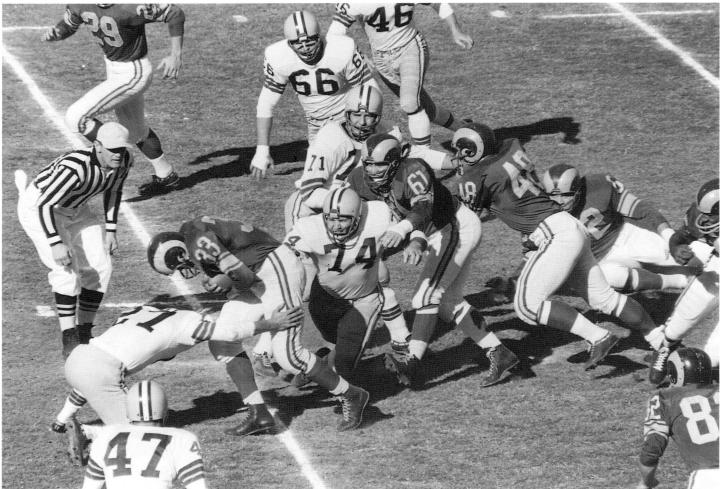

Opposite above: *Ollie Matson (right) holds a bronze medal won at the 1952 Helsinki Olympics in the 400-meter dash. Jamaicans Herb McKinney (left) and V. G. Rhoden (center) won silver and gold, respectively. Matson also brought home the gold as a member of the winning 1,600-meter relay team. Matson then reported to the Chicago Cardinals' training camp and ran away from most NFL defenders.*

Opposite below: *Matson (pictured wearing 33 for the Los Angeles Rams), with his sprinter's speed and 210 pounds, was coveted by every NFL team. The Rams sent nine players to the Cards for him in 1959.*

Left: *Deacon Dan Towler, out of tiny Washington & Jefferson via Stan Musial's hometown of Donora, Pennsylvania, came to the Rams in 1950 and banged away at opposing lines for the next six seasons. He used his pro football salary to finance his divinity school studies, and today is an ordained minister. Towler led the NFL in rushing in 1952.*

Page 80 above: *There have been faster runners, and more powerful runners – but no one ran "prettier" than Hugh "the King" McElhenny (39) of the San Francisco 49ers, with the possible exception of Gale Sayers. McElhenny evades Bears Stan Wallace and John Kreamcheck (facemask).*

Page 80 below: *Wearing a lucite mask to protect an injured face, Joe "the Jet" Perry of the 49ers is about to use his afterburners on the Packers' Ben Aldridge. With Perry and McElhenny in the same backfield, the 49ers' opponents had nightmares.*

Page 81 above: *Rick Casares (35) of the Bears typified the rough, tough image of George Halas's Monsters of the Midway. The 225-pound bulldozer was not only a 1,000-yard rusher, he could block with chilling effect.*

Page 81 below: *Most of Tony Canadeo's (3) great work for the Packers was in the forties – like 1,052 yards in '49 – but "the Gray Ghost of Gonzaga" continued to produce into the fifties.*

MANY HAPPY RETURNS
Kick Returners

Average of NFL Kickoff Returns by Decade – Showing How as Return Specialists Evolved in the 1960s, Special Teams Coaching Improved to Keep Pace and Lower the Average Return

Decade	No. of Leaders' Returns	Yards per Return Average
1940s	159	26.8
1950s	155	32.0
1960s	225	33.1
1970s	212	30.6
1980s	298	28.6
1990s	160	25.8

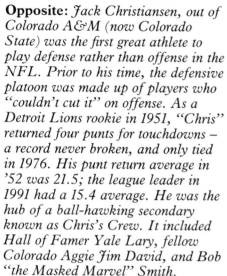

Opposite: *Jack Christiansen, out of Colorado A&M (now Colorado State) was the first great athlete to play defense rather than offense in the NFL. Prior to his time, the defensive platoon was made up of players who "couldn't cut it" on offense. As a Detroit Lions rookie in 1951, "Chris" returned four punts for touchdowns – a record never broken, and only tied in 1976. His punt return average in '52 was 21.5; the league leader in 1991 had a 15.4 average. He was the hub of a ball-hawking secondary known as Chris's Crew. It included Hall of Famer Yale Lary, fellow Colorado Aggie Jim David, and Bob "the Masked Marvel" Smith.*

Above and Above right: *This two-picture sequence shows just how swiftly Christiansen (24) could strike. The first shot shows him taking the opening kickoff of the 1956 Pro Bowl three yards deep in the end zone. The second shows him getting underway and upfield on a 103-yard touchdown. So, with about 15 seconds gone, Christiansen's West squad was up 6-0.*

Right: *Jon Arnett (26) of the Los Angeles Rams, known as "the Jaguar" because of his uncanny balance and cat-like moves, was as dangerous late in the decade as Christiansen was early in the fifties. On this play in 1959, against Vince Lombardi's first Packers team, he is in the initial stages of an 80-yard scoring punt return. Arnett was an accomplished gymnast and used that ability on the football field. He played in five consecutive Pro Bowls – 1958-62.*

DECADE HIGHLIGHTS

DECADE LEADERS, 1950s – NFL

PASSING
Yardage: Norm Van Brocklin · 20,539
Completion Percentage: Otto Graham · 55.7%
Touchdowns: Bobby Layne · 151
RUSHING
Yardage: Joe Perry · 7,151
Per Carry Average: Dan Towler · 5.2 yards
Touchdowns: Joe Perry · 49
RECEIVING
Receptions: Billy Wilson · 404
Yardage: Billy Howton · 6,091 yards
Per Catch Average: Ray Renfro · 20.5 yards
Touchdowns: Elroy "Crazylegs" Hirsch · 49
SCORING: Lou Groza · 742 points
PUNT RETURN AVERAGE: Billy Grimes · 13.2 yards
KICKOFF RET. AVE.: Lynn Chandnois · 29.6 yards
FIELD GOALS: Lou Groza · 131
PUNTING AVERAGE: Pat Brady · 44.5 yards
INTERCEPTIONS: Emlen Tunnell · 59

Opposite: *In 1953 Harlon Hill (left) played for Florence State Teachers College in Alabama. In 1954 he was NFL Rookie of the Year as he led the Chicago Bears with 45 catches for 1,124 yards and led the league with a 25-yard average per catch. In 1955 he was the NFL's Most Valuable Player – the trophy is presented here. When he retired after the 1962 season, he had the highest per-catch average in history – 20.2 yards. He was typical of the Bears' small-college, "sleeper" draft choices of the era.*

Right: *Dick "Night Train" Lane (in Chicago Cardinals white helmet) barely even played small college football – just a season at Scottsbluff J.C. As a rookie, he set a still-standing NFL record of 12 interceptions. He got his nickname as a rookie because he would often go to Tom Fears's room at training camp and ask to hear Buddy Morrow's great record of the bluesy hit of the day – "Night Train." Fears would look up and remark, "Here comes 'Night Train.'" Lane, later a bone-rattling, gambling defensive back with the Lions, is said to have "written the book on cornerbacking."*

Right below: *Sammy Baugh still has his supporters as the greatest passer ever. The tall, lean Texan from TCU arranges a program from each season he played with the Washington Redskins – 1937-52.*

Buddy Parker's (Detroit Lions) Record vs. Pro Football Hall of Fame Coach Paul Brown (Cleveland Browns) – 10-1-1		
PRESEASON		
Year	**Location**	**Score**
1951	Detroit	Detroit 21-Cleveland 20
1952	Syracuse, NY	Detroit 28-Cleveland 21
1953	Detroit	Detroit 24-Cleveland 24
1954	Dallas	Detroit 56-Cleveland 31
1955	Cleveland	Detroit 19-Cleveland 3
1956	Detroit	Detroit 17-Cleveland 0
1956	Akron, OH	Detroit 31-Cleveland 14
REGULAR SEASON		
1952	Detroit	Detroit 17-Cleveland 6
1954	Cleveland	Detroit 14-Cleveland 10
NFL CHAMPIONSHIPS		
1952	Detroit	Detroit 17-Cleveland 7
1953	Detroit	Detroit 17-Cleveland 6
1954	Cleveland	Cleveland 56-Detroit 10

Opposite: *Doak Walker, Bobby Layne's high school and pro teammate (Detroit Lions), was a great clutch performer. Layne said, "Ahead 20-0, Doak wasn't worth a damn, but at 7-7 or 13-14, with little time left, he would do the unbelievable." Walker returned the compliment, saying, "Ol' Bobby never lost a game, but once in a while he ran out of time." Walker and Layne are enshrined in Canton.*

Right: *After laying waste to the AAFC, the Cleveland Browns swept the league title in their first season in the NFL – 1950. Coach Paul Brown (left) and owner Mickey McBride (right) congratulate Lou Groza, who kicked the winning field goal to edge the Rams 30-28.*

Below: *Buddy Parker, being given the traditional coach's victory ride by his Detroit Lions players, Gus Cifelli (left) and Bob Smith, after the 1952 NFL Championship Game, would band a group of Texans together to form the nucleus of the dominant team of the fifties.*

The 1960s

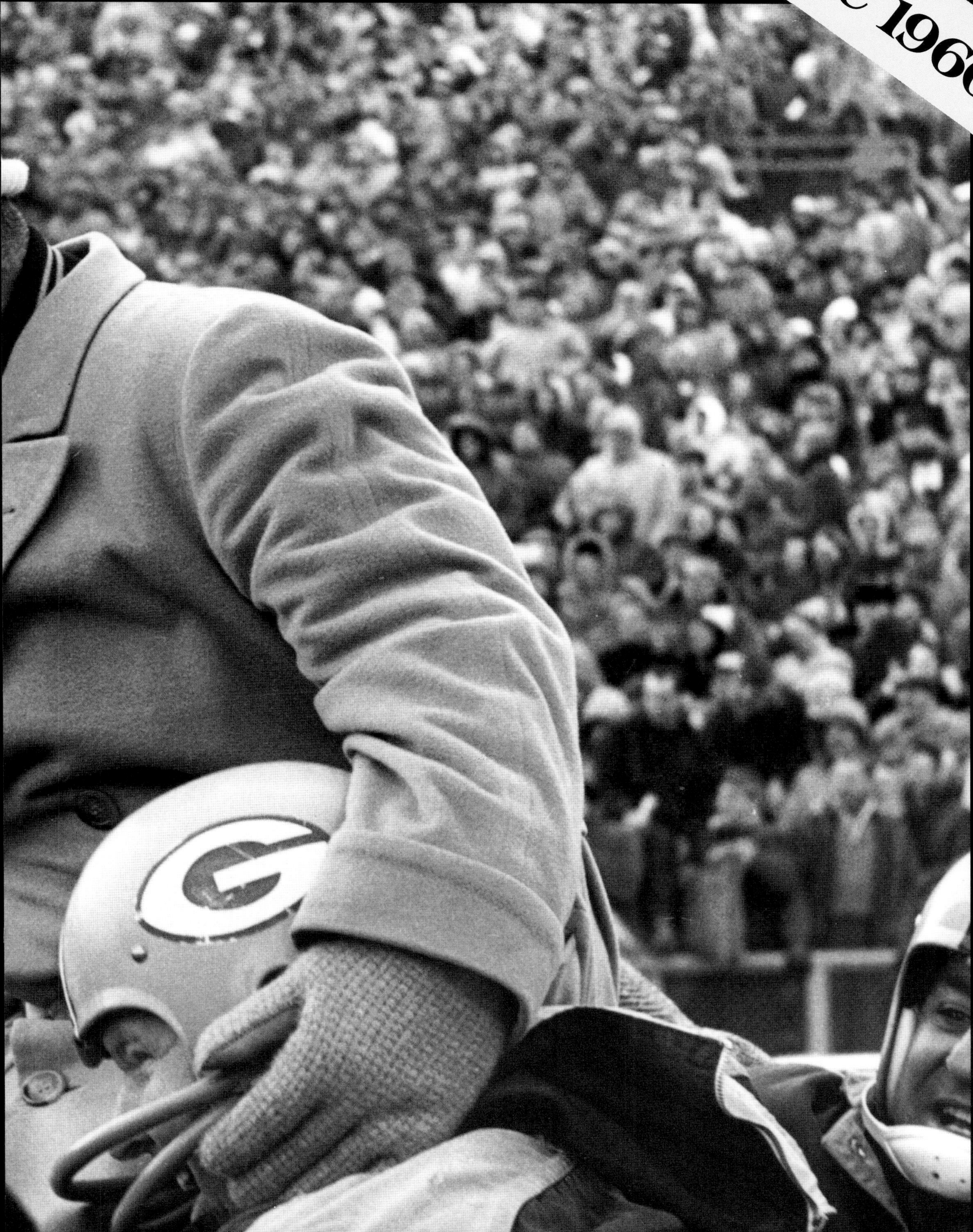

As was the case when the AAFC challenged the NFL in the 1940s, with the 1960s challenge of the American Football League the players benefited and the owners bemoaned their collective loss. Not only were more jobs available in pro football, they also paid much better. The Other League, as NFL hardcores called it, not only provided paychecks, but gave job opportunities to such players as a 200-pound center (Jim Otto from the University of Miami), a somewhat slow but sure-handed defensive back-turned-receiver (Lionel Taylor from New Mexico Highlands), and a 5'6", 162-pound kick returner (Jack Larschied from the College of the Pacific).

Two young Texas sportsmen, whose families had struck it rich in oil, K.S. "Bud" Adams, Jr. and Lamar Hunt, were tired of being rejected in bids for NFL franchises. So they did the next best thing. With the help of a few others, they started the AFL – formed in late 1959 to begin play in 1960. The new league brought pro football to Houston, Buffalo again, Boston again, Denver and Oakland.

For the most part, in the early years of the decade the NFL won the signing wars between the leagues as they both vied for player talent. Some individual teams in the AFL were successful, but on the whole the NFL got most of the players it wanted. This would change.

In 1959 the brightest stars of the NFL – Johnny Unitas and Norm Van Brocklin to name a pair – were making about $25,000 a year. And that was thought to be big money. The AFL changed all that, leading up to the signing of Joe Namath for an unfathomable $409,000-deal in 1965.

Something had to be done, especially after newly-appointed AFL Commissioner Al Davis began signing the top NFL stars (translate that as quarterbacks) to future contracts with the AFL. Largely through the negotiations of NFL representative Tex Schramm and AFL rep Lamar Hunt, a merger between the two pro leagues was announced on June 8, 1966. It would provide for a combined draft with no more bidding wars, a combined league of 24 teams under one banner, and an AFL-NFL Championship Game (later known as the Super Bowl) starting in January of 1967.

The merger, if it didn't save both leagues, at least saved certain franchises. The bidding for players was going out of sight. In the early years, a colleague of legendary oil wildcatter H.L. Hunt (Lamar's father), said to the elder Hunt, "Do you know Lamar is losing $1,000,000 a year on that damn fool football team?" Hunt is said to have replied, "In that case, the boy will be broke in a hundred-fifty-eight years."

The cost of operating a pro football franchise in the sixties was climbing, but that didn't stop all from joining in. The NFL expanded to Dallas in 1960 and Minnesota in 1961. The Atlanta Falcons and New Orleans Saints joined later in the decade.

Once the Chargers moved from Los Angeles to San Diego and the Dallas Texans became the Kansas City Chiefs, the AFL was stabilized until expansion late in the decade. The Miami Dolphins and Cincinnati Bengals began play in 1966 and 1968, respectively.

Television continued to sweeten the pot for pro football as rights fees increased with each new contract. TV was paying the freight, but pro football was satisfying a public demand on the medium. Both the NFL (on CBS) and the AFL (on NBC) had total network packages. All teams shared equally in the revenue from the TV deals. After the merger brought about an integrated playing schedule, ABC would also join in.

Two other things that hardly caused a ripple took place in the sixties, and each would impact greatly on the next decade. On Monday night, October 31, 1966, the Chicago Bears played the St. Louis Cardinals in St. Louis. The game was televised nationally in prime time, and although nothing came of it at the time, it proved to be an idea ahead of its time. Equally without fanfare, NFL Properties was organized in the early 1960s. Originally meant to be a quality-control operation, NFLP mushroomed into a tremendous money-maker as it licensed the manufacture of everything from team caps to team sneakers, with belt buckles, pennants, thermal mugs and frisbees in between.

On the playing field, the Packers, under Vince Lombardi, emerged as a dynasty; the Steelers, under a succession of coaches, would challenge the expansion Falcons

and Saints for the dubious distinction as worst team of the decade. The status quo would not remain in place for very long.

As a sport, pro football was quickly becoming the "most followed" by American males aged 18 to 49. This fact would not be lost on TV network executives and advertising agency heads. Attendance climbed steadily at the stadium. The average NFL crowd in 1969 was 54,430.

The sixties may have been turbulent for the United States and the world in general, but under the leadership of Pete Rozelle, the NFL was about to enter the 1970s on a solid footing.

With some financial inducement, the Pittsburgh Steelers, Cleveland Browns and Baltimore Colts would join former AFL teams in forming the American Football Conference of the restructured NFL.

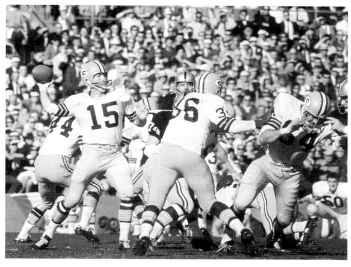

Pages 88-89: *Vince Lombardi (atop players' shoulders) tastes the first of many NFL championships as his Green Bay Packers shut out the Giants, 37-0, on the last day of 1961.*

Opposite left: *The New York Giants of the fifties and early sixties were in six NFL title games. Unfortunately, they would win only one, in 1956, but their success in the media/advertising capital of New York at the time did much to advance the cause of pro football.*

Opposite right: *Joe Namath, shown as an AFL-New York Jets rookie in 1965, would evolve into the legendary "Broadway Joe" just as the NFL Giants were going into decline. The brash rookie, with his $409,000 contract – then a staggering sum – and his fondness for bright lights and blonds, would become a spokesperson for many in the sixties.*

Above right: *Quarterback Bart Starr (15) of the Packers readies to pass from a protective pocket. In contrast to the flamboyant Namath, Starr was a cool, calculating extension of his coach – Vince Lombardi – once he took the field to direct the Pack's considerable arsenal of offensive weaponry. From the Packers' offensive platoon of the sixties, tackle Forrest Gregg, halfback Paul Hornung, center Jim Ringo, Starr, and fullback Jim Taylor are Pro Football Hall of Famers. Naturally, their coach is, too.*

DECADE STANDINGS – 1960s
American Football League

Team	W-L-T	Percentage
Dallas Texans/Kansas City Chiefs[1]	87-48-5	.639
Los Angeles/San Diego Chargers[2]	86-48-6	.636
Oakland Raiders[3]	77-58-5	.568
Houston Oilers[4]	70-66-4	.514
New York Titans/Jets[5]	69-65-6	.514
Buffalo Bills[6]	65-69-6	.486
Boston Patriots	63-68-9	.482
Denver Broncos	39-97-4	.293
Miami Dolphins	15-39-2	.286
Cincinnati Bengals	7-20-1	.268

[1] won AFL titles in 1962, 1966 and 1969; won SB IV.
[2] won AFL title in 1963.
[3] won AFL title in 1967.
[4] won AFL titles in 1960 and 1961.
[5] won AFL title in 1968; won SB III.
[6] won AFL titles in 1964 and 1965.

DECADE STANDINGS – 1960s NFL

Team	W-L-T	Percentage
Green Bay Packers[1]	96-37-5	.714
Cleveland Browns[2]	92-41-5	.685
Baltimore Colts[3]	92-42-4	.681
New York Giants	69-63-6	.522
Detroit Lions	66-61-11	.518
St. Louis Cardinals	67-65-8	.514
Chicago Bears[4]	67-65-6	.507
Dallas Cowboys	67-65-6	.507
Los Angeles Rams	63-68-7	.482
Minnesota Vikings[5]	52-67-7	.440
San Francisco 49ers	57-74-7	.438
Philadelphia Eagles[6]	57-76-5	.431
Washington Redskins	46-82-10	.370
Pittsburgh Steelers	46-85-7	.359
New Orleans Saints	12-29-1	.298
Atlanta Falcons	12-43-1	.223

[1] won NFL titles in 1961, 1962, 1965, 1966 and 1967; won SB I and SB II.
[2] won NFL title in 1964
[3] won NFL title in 1968.
[4] won NFL title in 1963.
[5] won NFL title in 1969.
[6] won NFL title in 1960.

THE OTHER LEAGUE
The American Football League

**Nineteen Men Who Played All Ten Seasons of the
American Football League – 1960-69**

Player/Position	Team/Years
George Blanda/QB-K	Houston/1960-66
	Oakland/1967-69
Billy Cannon/RB-TE	Houston/1960-62
	Oakland/1963-69
Gino Cappelletti/WR-K	Boston/1960-69
Larry Grantham/LB	New York/1960-69
Wayne Hawkins/G	Oakland/1960-69
Jim "Earthquake"	
Hunt/DT	Boston/1960-69
Harry Jacobs/LB	Boston/1960-62
	Buffalo/1963-69
Jack Kemp/QB	Los Angeles-San Diego/1960-62
	Buffalo/1962-69
Paul Lowe/RB	Los Angeles-San Diego/1960-68
	Kansas City/1968-69
Jacky Lee/QB	Houston/1960-63 and 1966-67
	Denver/1964-65
	Kansas City/1967-69
Bill Mathis/FB	New York/1960-69
Paul Maguire/LB-P	Los Angeles-San Diego/1960-63
	Buffalo/1964-69
Don Maynard/WR	New York/1960-69
Ron Mix/T	Los Angeles-San Diego/1960-69
Jim Otto/C	Oakland/1960-69
Babe Parilli/QB	Oakland/1960
	Boston/1961-67
	New York/1968-69
Johnny Robinson/RB-S	Dallas-Kansas City/1960-69
Paul "Rocky"	
Rochester/DT	Dallas-Kansas City/1960-63
	New York/1963-69
Ernie Wright/T	Los Angeles-San Diego/1960-67
	Cincinnati/1968-69

Opposite above: *While this 1962 AFL shot depicts the Denver Broncos in action – that's veteran quarterback Frank Tripucka (18) about to launch a pass toward Gene Prebola (not pictured) – the reader is spared the ordeal of having to see the Broncs' infamous vertically-striped stockings. With a 7-7 record, Denver's Jack Faulkner was named AFL Coach of the Year.*

Opposite below: *Lance Alworth (19) caught only a handful of passes as a running back at Arkansas, but his acrobatic and athletic skills were so great with the San Diego Chargers (1962-70) that he became the first "homegrown" American Football League player elected to the Pro Football Hall of Fame. Alworth's boyish looks and great leaping ability earned him the nickname "Bambi," a tag of which he was not especially fond.*

Left above: *Jack Kemp (15) may be more visible today as a politician, but in the sixties he was an upper echelon quarterback with the Chargers and Buffalo Bills (shown here as the Bills played the AFL All-Stars after the 1965 season). Kemp leaps to escape Chargers defensive end Earl Faison. Kemp jokingly told his upstate New York constituents, "Vote for me, or I'll come back and quarterback the Bills." He won several terms in the U.S. House of Representatives before becoming a Cabinet member. Kemp's son Jeff followed him into the NFL as a quarterback.*

Left below: *George Blanda (16) led the Houston Oilers to the first two AFL Championships (1960, 1961), and narrowly missed the third in double-overtime. Blanda typified the early AFL stars in that he and they were usually recycled NFL players. Blanda first joined the NFL with the Bears in 1949. He went to "the other league" – NFL purists couldn't bring themselves to mention the AFL by name – in 1960.*

Pages 94-95: *By 1969, when this action – featuring the Oakland Raiders' George Atkinson (43) – took place, the AFL was truly a viable entity, and would merge playing-schedules with the NFL for the 1970 season.*

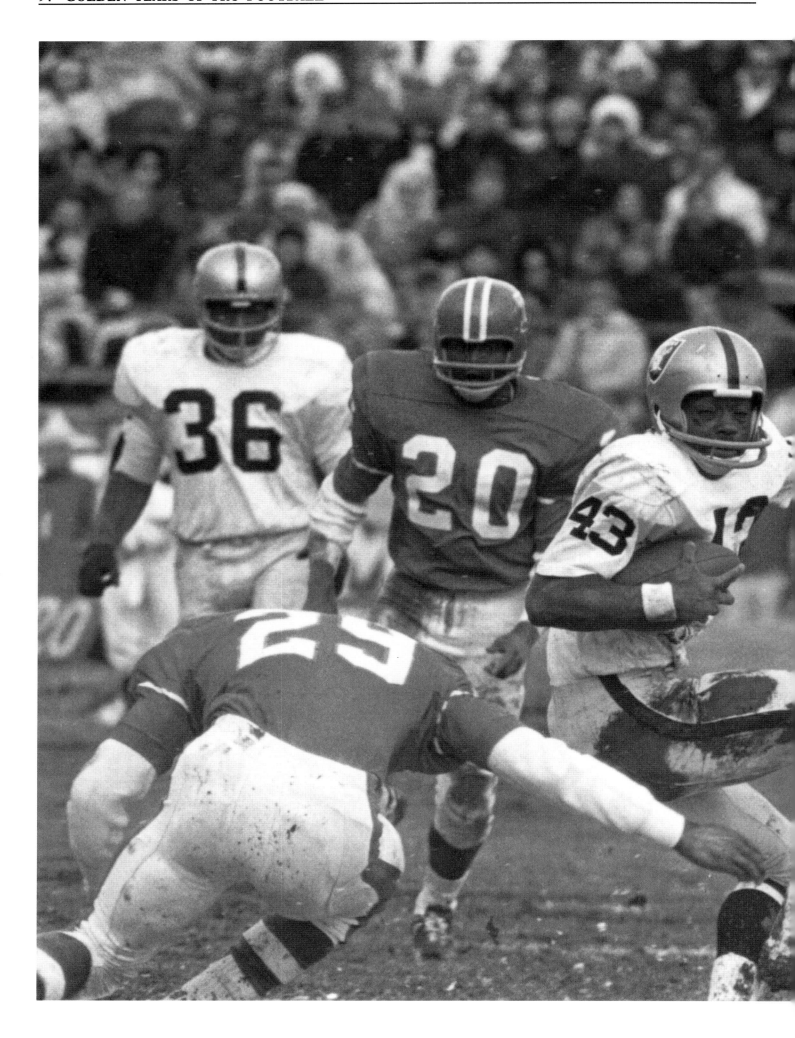

PHILLY FLYERS
The 1960 Eagles

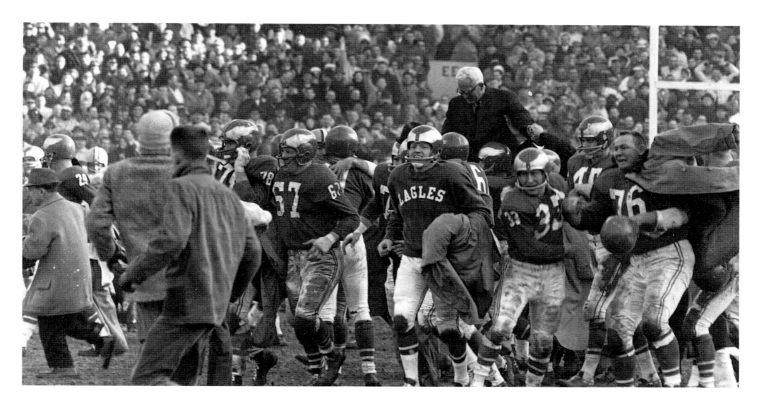

Opposite above: *The Philadelphia Eagles of 1960 had what was probably only the third-best personnel in the NFL East, but that didn't stop them from winning the NFL Championship. Here, diminutive (5' 9", 176 lbs.) receiver Tommy McDonald is offered police protection as he attempts to rejoin his mates after taking a 35-yard touchdown pass from Norm Van Brocklin in second-quarter play of the title game.*

Opposite below: *Ted Dean (35), a rookie Philadelphian, ignited the Eagles with a long kickoff return made possible when assistant Charlie Gauer spotted a weakness in the Packers' coverage. Here he scores the winning touchdown in the 17-13 game to clinch the NFL title.*

Above: *Coach Buck Shaw, who would retire after the game as the only man to defeat Vince Lombardi in a championship game, is escorted from the field by his players, including Stan Campbell (67), Sonny Jurgensen (in Eagles warmup), Billy Ray Barnes (33), Don Burroughs (45) and J. D. Smith (76).*

Right: *The catalyst for the Eagles was Norm Van Brocklin, traded from the Rams in 1958. Alex Karras said it, and it's probably true, "No one ever played quarterback like the Dutchman did in 1960."*

AIRBORNE
Quarterbacks

Left: *Y. A. Tittle (white t-shirt) may have been the best quarterback to never win an NFL Championship. He took his New York Giants to three straight title games, 1961-63, but couldn't clear the last hurdle. That did not keep him from the Pro Football Hall of Fame. Shown with him are teammates (left to right) Jerry Hillebrand, Joe Morrison and Frank Gifford. Tittle, who had a rocky start, rallied to throw four touchdowns to defeat the 49ers – his old team – this day, and get a leg up in the NFL East as they drove for the 1963 division title.*

Below: *Gifford, retired by now, interviews winning quarterback Len Dawson after Super Bowl IV.*

Opposite: *Sonny Jurgensen (9), in action against the Steelers in 1969, moved from the Eagles to the Washington Redskins in an earlier controversial trade for quarterback Norm Snead. The portly passer became a true capital asset and is said to have been the best "pure passer" the game has ever seen. His arm was tireless, as he threw for 32,224 yards and 255 touchdowns – an amazing total when taken into consideration he understudied Norm Van Brocklin in Philadelphia as he threw as few as five passes in some seasons. In his first year as a fulltime starter, 1961, he set NFL records for completions (235), yards (3723), and touchdowns (32).*

1965 NFL Team Standings with Pass:Run Ratios (Rankings in Parentheses)		
Team/W-L-T	Rushing Attempts (Rank)	Pass Attempts (Rank)
Browns/11-3-0	412 (9)	419 (4)
Colts/10-3-1	410 (10)	400 (5)
Packers/10-3-1	480 (3)	383 (8)
Bears/9-5-0	400 (14)	444 (2)
49ers/7-6-1	405 (13)	448 (1)
Cowboys/7-7-0	422 (6)	426 (3)
Vikings/7-7-0	408 (12)	357 (10)
Giants/7-7-0	447 (4)	393 (6)
Lions/6-7-1	409 (11)	344 (13)
Redskins/6-8-0	486 (1)	318 (14)
Eagles/5-9-0	419 (7)	393 (7)
Cardinals/5-9-0	433 (5)	380 (9)
Rams/4-10-0	417 (8)	349 (12)
Steelers/2-12-0	483 (2)	353 (11)

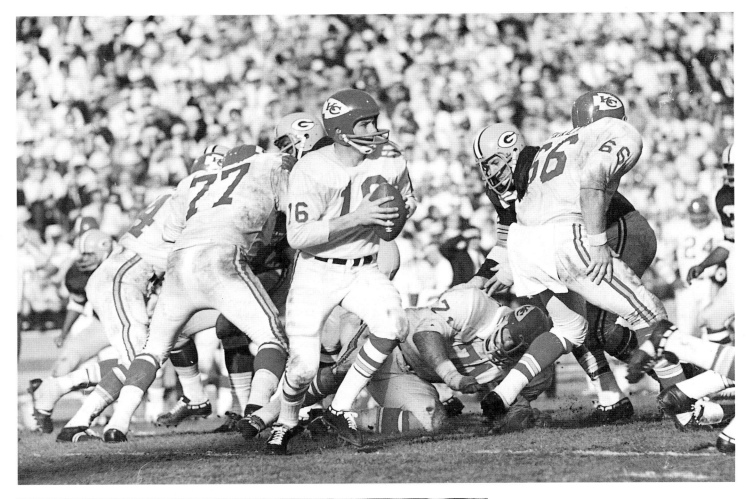

Above: *Len Dawson (16) would see his Purdue All-America skills erode as he rode the bench with a couple of NFL teams, but would find a home and stardom in the AFL with the Dallas Texans, who then became the Kansas City Chiefs. Perhaps his finest performance was in Super Bowl IV, when he completed 12 of 17 passes for 142 yards and one TD to defeat the favored Minnesota Vikings.*

Left: *Greg Cook burst onto the AFL scene with his hometown Cincinnati Bengals in 1969, after leading the nation in total offense (3,210 yards) at the University of Cincinnati in 1968. He led the AFL in passing as a rookie, but missed the entire seasons of 1970 and '71 with an arm injury. He ended his career in 1972. There is no doubt that, if healthy, he would have ranked with the finest ever.*

Opposite: *Fran Tarkenton (10) is best remembered for his early scrambling with the Minnesota Vikings and later leading them to three Super Bowls, but in between he did time in New York with the Giants, 1967-71.*

STICKY FINGERS
Receivers

Opposite: *Don Maynard (13), the lanky, eccentric, elusive wideout from Texas Western (now UTEP), was as feared as any receiver in pro football. Often he was on the other end of Joe Namath's guided missiles. This catch scored the New York Jets' winning touchdown in the 1968 AFL championship. The Jets would then go on to rock the pro football world in Super Bowl III – upsetting the Colts.*

Above: *Bobby Mitchell (49) was a track star (a sprinter, not a hurdler) who could do it all on a football field. Here with the Cleveland Browns in 1961 in a game against his future team – the Washington Redskins – he makes big yardage. Mitchell was primarily a kick returner and runner in Cleveland. It was in Washington that he blossomed into a Hall of Fame receiver – finishing his career in 1968 with 521 catches for 7,954 yards. Mitchell scored 65 touchdowns receiving, 18 rushing, and 8 on kick returns.*

Right: *John Mackey (88) was a prototype tight end. He was big, fast, powerful, had great hands, refused to be tackled by one man, and blocked like a demon. An oft-shown film clip shows him scoring after being hemmed in by six Lions defenders. Thought of by some as a rebel because of his players' union activities, Mackey took his rightful place in Canton in 1992.*

THE LAST HURRAH
Halas's Last Championship, 1963

Opposite above: *In many ways to many people, George Halas (right, with star Red Grange in the 1920s) was the NFL. He was there at the beginning in Canton, and he was there at the end – continuing to work for his Chicago Bears until his death in 1983. While he is best remembered as an owner/coach, Halas was the Bears' right end through 1929. He once held the NFL record for the longest return of a fumble – 98 yards.*

Opposite below: *Sid Luckman and Halas look on approvingly as the Bears dismantle the Redskins, 73-0, in the 1940 championship game – one of six NFL titles won by Halas's Bears.*

Left: *Halas and his team brave the snowy weather on the sidelines. The Hall of Fame coach's 325 NFL victories are still the record.*

Page 106: *Halas and the Bears defeated the Giants, 14-10, on a blustery day in the Windy City for the 1963 NFL Championship. Typically for the Bears, it was the defense that carried the day. Here defensive end Ed O'Bradovich (87) intercepts a Giants' screen pass on their 20 and returns it to their 14. With the Bears trailing, 10-7, in the third period, this set up the Chicagoans' second and winning touchdown. O'Bradovich eludes Giants tackle Jack Stroud (66).*

Page 107 above: *Bill Wade (9) was no exponent of the vertical passing game, but his ball control, short passes, mixed with screens and draws, were enough to put the Bears on top for the season and in the '63 title game. Here, Herman Lee (70), Bob Wetoska (63), and Joe Marconi (34) impede the progress of John LoVetere (76, partially hidden) and Jim Katcavage (75).*

Page 107 below: *You have to take our word for it, but Wade (9, far left) scores on this play for his second TD, shortly after O'Bradovich's interception. Blocking are: Mike Pyle (50), Ted Karras (67, nearly hidden), and Herman Lee (70). Futile Giants defenders include John LoVetere (76) and Sam Huff (white jersey, partially visible behind LoVetere).*

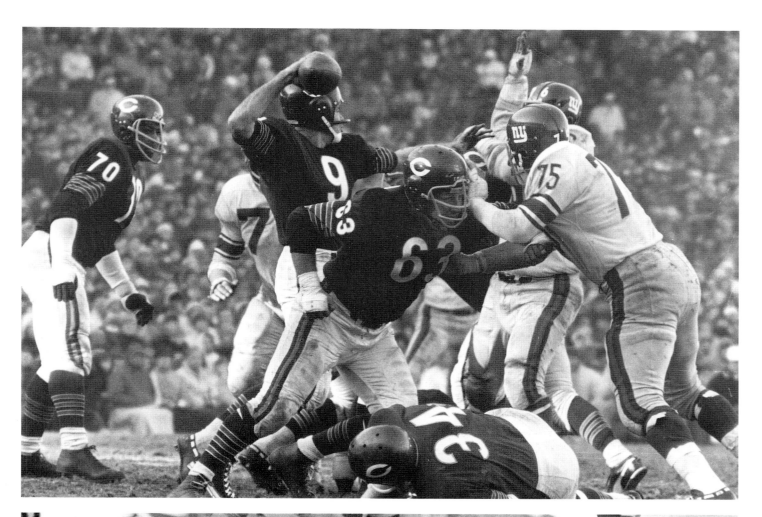

GO WEST, YOUNG MAN!
Early Cowboys

Opposite: *Long before the Dallas Cowboys were America's Team, they were just an expansion team, taking their lumps in the early 1960s. Tom Landry, their first and only coach until 1989, shows a play diagram to runners (left to right) Don Perkins, J. W. Lockett and Amos Marsh.*

Above: *A gripping 1963 confrontation between two future Hall of Famers – the Cowboys' Bob Lilly (74) and Giants quarterback Y. A. Tittle. Lilly, of whom Landry said, "A player like Lilly comes along once in a coach's lifetime," got by Jack Stroud (66). Off to the left, John Meyers (78) and Greg Larson (53) spar for position.*

Right: *In a 1963 game Don Perkins (43) eludes the Eagles' George Tarasovic, who joined the team too recently to have the Eagles' wing affixed to his helmet. Perkins was a workhorse for the Cowboys until additional talent arrived in the late sixties. Perkins, a compact 200-pounder, took a hammering, but when asked by quarterback Don Meredith "Can you still go?" simply answered, "Yeah, I can run," and whanged into the opposing line. Perkins was as underrated and under-appreciated as anyone who ever played in the NFL.*

BROWN & ASSOCIATES
Great Runners

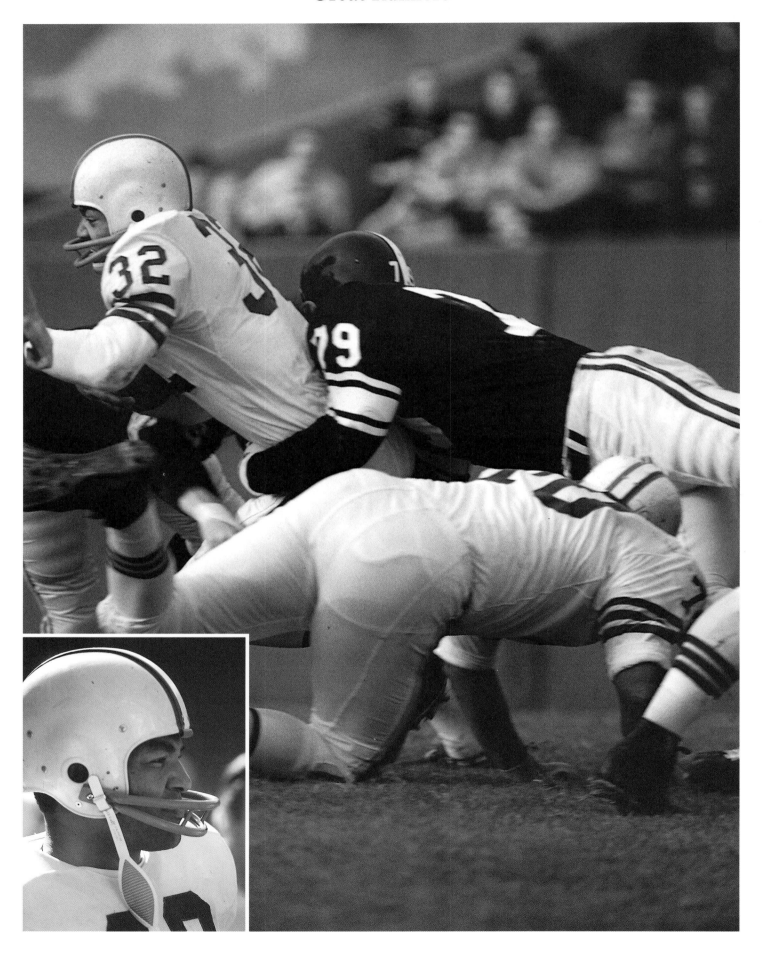

Opposite and Inset: *If the criteria for a running back is running with the football, then Jim Brown (32) of the Cleveland Browns is the best ever – end of discussion. No one was more consistent or more effective over the course of a career than Brown. He averaged more than 100 yards a game every season. His per-carry average (5.2 yards) is highest by far of any longtime running back. He led the league in rushing in all but one of his nine seasons. He was head and shoulders above the crowd.*

Above left: *When Brown remained in England shooting* The Dirty Dozen *in 1966, opponents did not get a break. Leroy Kelly (44) picked up where Brown left off, gaining more than 1,000 yards that year – a feat he would repeat often.*

Above right: *Before Earvin Johnson, Gale Sayers was "Magic." He had instinctive moves that were never surpassed and seldom duplicated. It was said that his rookie year (1965) performance, when he scored six touchdowns in a game against the 49ers, was like "a season's highlight film." Injuries robbed Sayers of his magical movement, but they couldn't keep him out of Canton.*

Jim Brown's Individual Rushing Statistics Compared to NFL Team Statistics – 1963

	Attempts	Yards	Average	Touchdowns
JIM BROWN	291	1,863	6.4	12
TEAM				
Minnesota	445	1,842	4.1	17
St. Louis	423	1,839	4.3	10
Dallas	420	1,795	4.3	18
New York Giants	453	1,777	3.9	12
Chicago	487	1,679	3.4	15
Baltimore	396	1,642	4.1	11
Detroit	415	1,601	3.9	11
San Francisco	406	1,454	3.6	8
Philadelphia	376	1,438	3.8	8
Los Angeles	405	1,393	3.4	14
Washington	344	1,289	3.7	15

The only teams Brown did not outrush were his own Cleveland Browns, the Green Bay Packers and Pittsburgh Steelers.

AFL-NFL Runners of 1962 with High Yardage and Low Scoring Contrasted with Low Yardage and High Scoring

HIGH YARDAGE/LOW SCORING			LOW YARDAGE/HIGH SCORING		
Name	Yards	TDs	Name	TDs	Yards
Joe Perry	359	0	Norm Snead	3	10
Wayne Crow	589	1	Johnny Green	3	35
Tommy Mason	740	2	Cotton Davidson	3	54
Ronnie Bull	363	1	Alex Hawkins	4	87
Curtis McClinton	604	2	Warren Rabb	3	77
Keith Lincoln	574	2	Bill Wade	5	146
Ron Burton	548	2	Charlie Johnson	3	138
Dick Bass	1,033	6	John David Crow	14	751
Billy Ray Barnes	492	3	Tom Moore	7	377
John H. Johnson	1,141	7	Billy Cannon	7	474

Left: *John David Crow (44) scores in a 1962 game against the Giants. Crow won the Heisman Trophy at Texas A&M in 1957 and became a stalwart with the Chicago, and later St. Louis, Cardinals. A big, powerful runner – he gained 1,071 yards with a 5.9 average in 1960 – Crow became a tight end late in his career, after being traded to the 49ers. Whether a running back or a tight end, John David had the ability to perform one duty that warms the hearts of coaches and teammates – block! He was a terror with or without the ball.*

Above: *Clem Daniels (36) is the correct answer to an incorrect trivia question: "Who were the most valuable players in 1963 of baseball's American and National leagues, the NFL, and the AFL, who all wore jersey No. 32?" The incorrect answer usually given is: Elston Howard, Sandy Koufax, Jim Brown and Cookie Gilchrist. Not! Gilchrist, who wore No. 34, was not the AFL's MVP. Daniels, who was, wore No. 36, as shown above. In this game against the New York Titans, the Raiders' Daniels is using John Kenerson (75) as a stepping stone into the Polo Grounds' end zone. Blocking is Alan Miller (37).*

RUSHERS, STUFFERS, AND BUSTERS

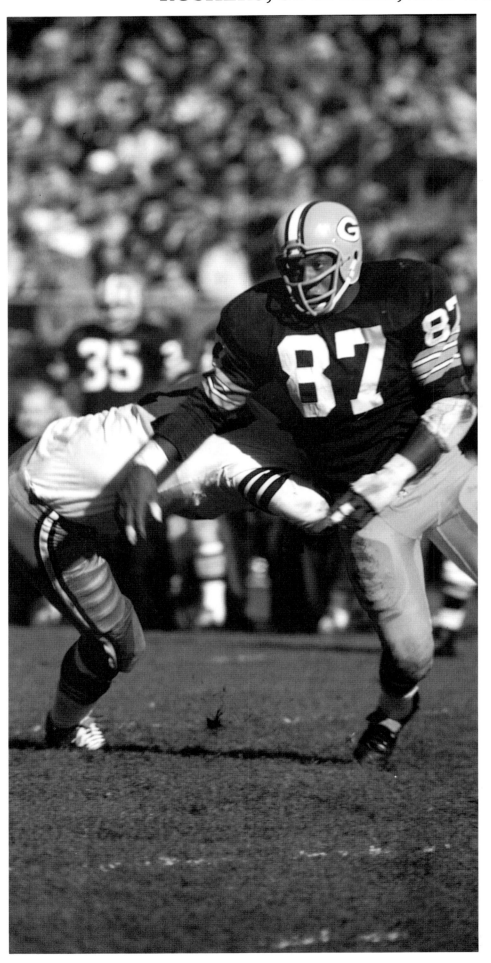

Left: *Willie Davis (87), with his eye on a Cowboys runner as he shucks a block, represented the defensive platoon of Lombardi's dynastic Green Bay Packers of the sixties. Davis left Grambling to join the Browns in 1958. In the steal of the century, he was traded to the Pack in 1960. Used as an offensive lineman for the Browns, Davis was converted to defensive end and turned loose by Lombardi. Davis, a Hall of Famer, played in 162 games in his 12-year career – that's all of them.*

Opposite above: *Andy Robustelli (81), with a little help from his New York Giants friend Sam Huff (70), finally stops Jim Brown (32). Robustelli began his career as a two-way end with the Rams in 1951. After the 1955 season, he requested and was granted a trade to the Giants. As he did with the Rams, he performed at a Pro Bowl level with his new team. Undersized at 6' 0", 235 pounds, Robustelli was relentless in his pursuit.*

Opposite below left: *By 1969, when this action took place, the Los Angeles Rams' Deacon Jones was among the most feared defenders in football. Able to give an all-out rush, because Merlin Olsen filled the hole next to him, Jones often nailed quarterbacks before they could throw. He says he coined the term "sack," and who would argue with the 6' 5", 250-pound product of Mississippi Vocational College? Jones was called "Secretary of Defense."*

Opposite below right: *Although he played for the Kansas City Chiefs, Junious "Buck" Buchanan changed the face of the Raiders. It is said that Raiders owner Al Davis drafted future Hall of Famers Art Shell and Gene Upshaw specifically to contend with the 6' 7", 285-pounder. Buchanan was the first player drafted by the AFL in 1963 – quite an honor for a lineman from Grambling.*

Pages 116-117: *Known as the Fearsome Foursome, these Rams (left to right) – Lamar Lundy, Roger Brown, Merlin Olsen and Jones – wreaked havoc in the late sixties.*

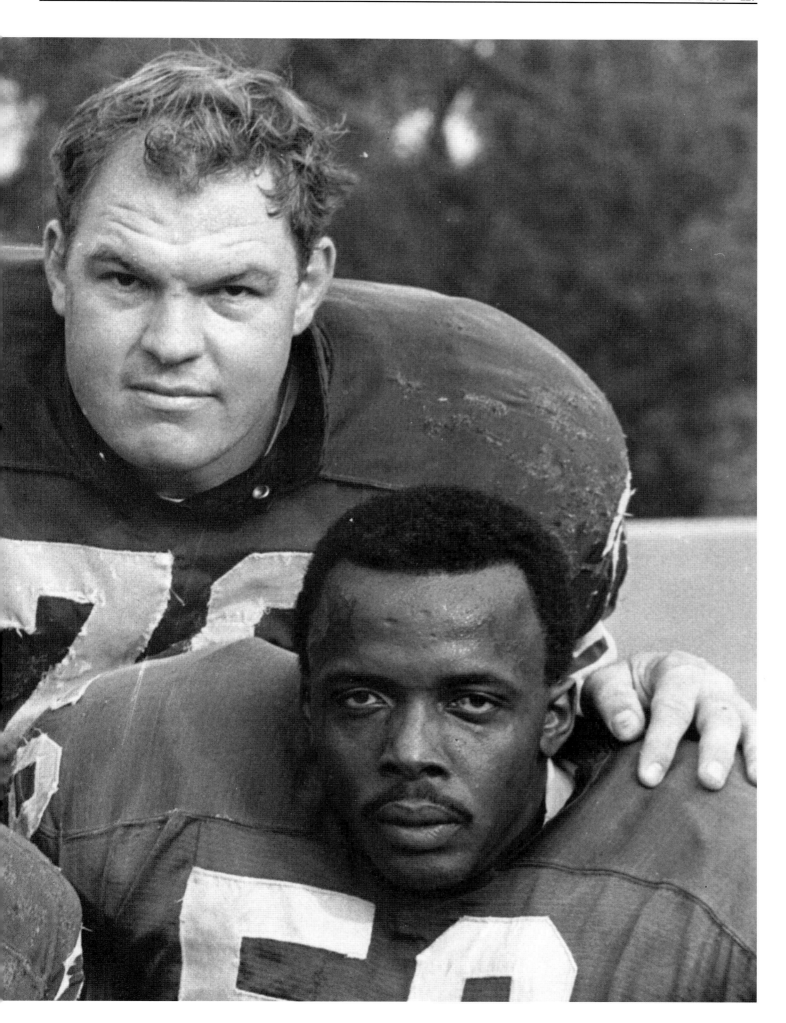

DYNASTY
Packers of the Sixties

Vince Lombardi's Post-season Record – 10-2-0

Year	Game	Score	Opposing Coach
1960	NFL Championship	Philadelphia 17-Green Bay 13	Buck Shaw
1961	NFL Championship	Green Bay 37-New York 0	Allie Sherman
1962	NFL Championship	Green Bay 16-New York 7	Allie Sherman
1963	Playoff Bowl	Green Bay 40-Cleveland 23	Blanton Collier
1964	Playoff Bowl	St. Louis 24-Green Bay 17	Wally Lemm
1965	Western Division Playoff	Green Bay 13-Baltimore 10	Don Shula
1965	NFL Championship	Green Bay 23-Cleveland 12	Blanton Collier
1966	NFL Championship	Green Bay 34-Dallas 27	Tom Landry
1966	Super Bowl I	Green Bay 35-Kansas City 10	Hank Stram
1967	Western Conference Championship	Green Bay 28-Los Angeles 7	George Allen
1967	NFL Championship	Green Bay 21-Dallas 17	Tom Landry
1967	Super Bowl II	Green Bay 33-Oakland 14	John Rauch

Opposite: *It was a scene that would be repeated often in the NFL in the sixties – Vince Lombardi and/or his Green Bay Packers celebrating still another victory. This one is over the Colts for the 1966 Western Division title.*

Above: *Although Lombardi didn't say so, Packers players sensed it would be his last game with them. Thus, they dedicated the second half of Super Bowl II "to the old man." It was his last game as Packers coach. Jerry Kramer provides the victory ride out of the Orange Bowl, January 14, 1968. Green Bay sent Oakland packing, 33-14.*

Right: *Bart Starr (15) was a doubtful starter for the Packers in the NFL Championship Game against the Browns on January 2, 1966, but he played well and the Packers won, 23-12. Starr listens intently to Lombardi.*

Opposite: *Starr was dangerous anytime he had the ball. At no time was he more dangerous than on "third and short." He would seemingly always "go deep" for a long gain.*

Right: *Paul Hornung, "the Golden Boy," was popular with Lombardi, the Packers, the fans and the ladies. Football's most eligible bachelor during his playing days, he was also a fine clutch performer. Eventually, he was inducted into the Pro Football Hall of Fame. His 176 points in 1960 is a single-season scoring record that may never be broken. Hornung, on a 2-8 Notre Dame team, won the 1956 Heisman Trophy, then languished until Lombardi arrived in '59 and said, "You're my left halfback."*

Below: *Jim Ringo was one of a handful of good players Lombardi inherited and made great. The undersized center (6' 1", 225 lbs.) joined the Pack in 1953 out of Syracuse.*

Below right: *Ray Nitschke (66) was a wildman when Lombardi arrived, but the coach channeled his ferocity and made him the most intimidating middle linebacker of his time.*

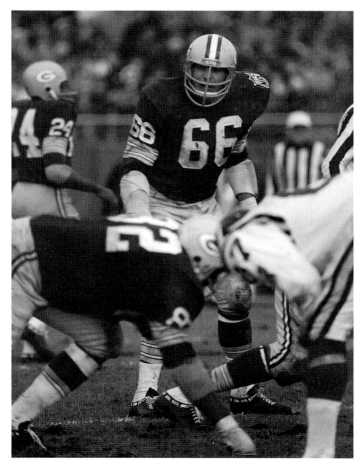

THE NAMATH EFFECT

Opposite: *With his rebel image and swinging lifestyle, Joe Namath of the New York Jets attracted, and affected, a whole new generation of fans. He was more than a figment of the New York media's imagination, too. Pro scouts, coaches and players will tell you he had "all the tools" of greatness.*

Above: *Namath (12) became an international star with his "guaranteed" victory over the Colts in Super Bowl III, pictured here. But he had help in this game from Emerson Boozer (32), Matt Snell, George Sauer and others.*

Right: *Namath, pictured in May of 1965 – before his rookie season – was also a man of myths. He is often cited as the first player taken in the 1965 AFL draft. Not so! That honor went to Baylor All-America wide receiver Lawrence Elkins. Namath, however, was second. Although injuries diminished Broadway Joe's skills and playing time, he was still a folk hero during and after his career. Making so many on the fringe aware of pro football would have been enough to get him to Canton.*

EQUALITY
The AFL Wins Two of Four AFL vs. NFL Super Bowls

Right: *The NFL and AFL squared off in four Super Bowls as separate leagues before the merged schedule of 1970. Each league won two games, so who's to say parity hadn't been reached? In Super Bowl I, the expressions of Kansas City's coach Hank Stram, an assistant, linebacker Smokey Stover (35), and Len Dawson (16) tell you as much as a scoreboard – Green Bay Packers 35-Kansas City Chiefs 10. Because no one knew if the TV blackout would or would not be in effect, and because it was the first Super Bowl (although it was officially called the AFL-NFL World Championship), the game was about 25,000 unsold tickets short of a sellout. It would be the only one that was not sold out.*

Opposite: *Green Bay's Max McGee (85), 34-year-old veteran who stayed out too late the night before with night owl Paul Hornung, did not expect to play much in Super Bowl I. However, starting wide receiver Boyd Dowler was injured early in the first quarter, and McGee was pressed into service. He rose to the occasion to catch 7 passes (he caught 6 all season) for 138 yards and 2 touchdowns. His first score (pictured en route here), naturally, represented the first points scored in Super Bowl history. McGee, never mistaken for Robert Redford, said of his running-mate Hornung, who could pass for a matinee idol – "With his charm and my looks, we can't miss."*

Comparison of the Five Leading Rushers and Passers of the AFL and the NFL in the 1960s

AFL Rushers		NFL Rushers	
Name	Yards	Name	Yards
Clem Daniels	5,101	Jim Brown	8,514
Paul Lowe	4,995	Jim Taylor	7,898
Abner Haynes	4,630	Don Perkins	6,217
Jim Nance	4,338	Dick Bass	5,417
Cookie Gilchrist	4,298	Bill Brown	4,868

AFL Passers		NFL Passers	
Jack Kemp	21,130	Johnny Unitas	26,548
George Blanda	20,029	Sonny Jurgensen	26,222
John Hadl	19,026	Fran Tarkenton	23,140
Len Dawson	18,899	John Brodie	22,196
Babe Parilli	18,289	Norm Snead	21,655

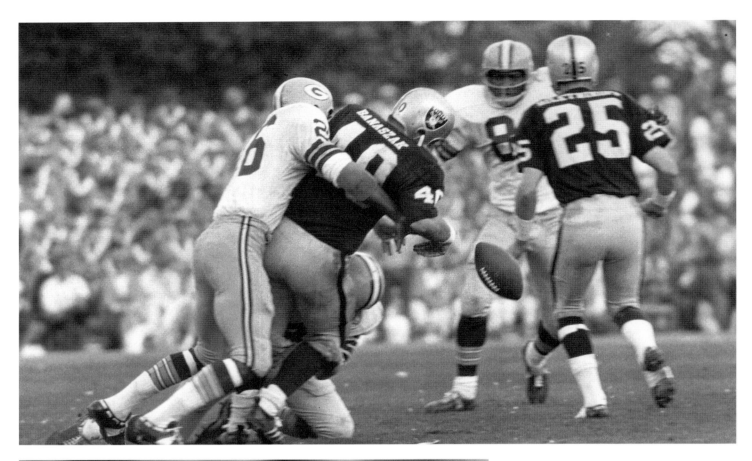

Above: *With the help of Herb Adderley (26, shaking the ball loose from Oakland Raiders Pete Banaszak), the Packers continued NFL mastery of the AFL by winning SB II, 33-14.*

Left: *By the time the Chiefs got back to the Super Bowl (SB IV), they were ready. Against the Vikings, the Super Chiefs were a formidable group. Len Dawson, under tremendous pressure from unsubstantiated rumors that he was friendly with a known gambler, responded with a class performance. However, the K.C. defense was just as important. Anchored by middle linebacker Willie Lanier (left), they completely shut down the Vikings. In the last Super Bowl between the NFL and AFL, the AFL Chiefs ambushed the Vikings, 23-17. It was the first of Minnesota's four Super Bowl defeats.*

Opposite: *Matt Snell, a two-way player at Ohio State under Woody Hayes, was projected by some in the New York Jets' organization as a linebacker. It's good they were voted down – Snell's 30 carries for 121 yards in SB III were a key to the Jets' stunning 16-7 upset of the Colts.*

DECADE HIGHLIGHTS

Left: *Lamar Hunt, frustrated by the NFL's denying him a franchise, did even better for himself. With a few friends, he formed the AFL. Hunt was the first AFL person to be elected to the Hall of Fame.*

Below: *As the commissioner of the AFL in 1966, Al Davis helped force the merger of the two leagues by signing the NFL's prime assets – its star quarterbacks – to future AFL contracts.*

Opposite: *Pete Rozelle (right, with officials of the Atlanta Athletic Association as they look at a proposed stadium site) became NFL commissioner in 1960 at age 33. For the next three decades, he led the NFL to unprecedented growth.*

DECADE LEADERS, 1960s – NFL

PASSING
Yardage: Johnny Unitas — 26,548
Completion Percentage: Bart Starr — 58.9%
Touchdowns: Sonny Jurgensen — 207
RUSHING
Yardage: Jim Brown — 8,514
Per Carry Average: Jim Brown — 5.3 yards
Touchdowns: Jim Taylor — 76
RECEIVING
Receptions: Bobby Mitchell — 470
Yardage: Bobby Mitchell — 7,472
Per Catch Average: Homer Jones — 22.6 yards
Touchdowns: Sonny Randle — 64
SCORING: Lou Michaels — 870 points
PUNT RETURN AVERAGE: Bob Hayes — 11.9 yards
KICKOFF RETURN AVERAGE: Gale Sayers — 30.6 yards
FIELD GOALS: Lou Michaels — 171
PUNTING AVERAGE: Yale Lary — 46.4 yards
INTERCEPTIONS: Bobby Boyd — 57

DECADE LEADERS, 1960s – AFL

PASSING
Yardage: Jack Kemp — 21,130
Completion Percentage: Len Dawson — 56.8%
Touchdowns: Len Dawson — 182
RUSHING
Yardage: Clem Daniels — 5,101
Per Carry Average: Paul Lowe — 4.9 yards
Touchdowns: Abner Haynes — 46
RECEIVING
Receptions: Lionel Taylor — 567
Yardage: Don Maynard — 10,289
Per Catch Average: Lance Alworth — 19.6 yards
Touchdowns: Don Maynard — 84
SCORING: Gino Cappelletti — 1,100 points
PUNT RETURN AVERAGE:
  Claude "Hoot" Gibson — 12.6 yards
KICKOFF RETURN AVERAGE: Bobby Jancik — 26.5
FIELD GOALS: Gino Cappelletti — 170
PUNTING AVERAGE: Jerrel Wilson — 43.9 yards
INTERCEPTIONS: Dave Grayson — 47

Above: *The war between the AFL and the NFL really got hot when Buffalo Bills soccer-style kicker Pete Gogolak (3) – the first of his kind – played out his option and joined the rival NFL Giants in 1966. Gogolak, with his family, escaped the Soviet takeover of Hungary in 1956, came to the U.S.A., and was graduated from Cornell before turning pro. His younger brother Charlie followed him to the Ivy League (Princeton) and to the NFL (Redskins).*

Left: *Tom Matte (with coach Don Shula, right) was forced to play quarterback for the Baltimore Colts in the 1965 Western Division playoff against the Packers. Matte, a quarterback at run-oriented Ohio State, was a halfback for several years with the Colts before injuries to Johnny Unitas and Gary Cuozzo caused the switch. To help him, Matte wore a wristband on which the team's plays were written.*

Opposite: *Matte, in his more conventional role, was a productive running back despite Alex Karras calling him "a garbage can runner." Matte had little dash and flash, but was reliable. In Cleveland Matte scored thrice as the Colts won the 1968 NFL title game.*

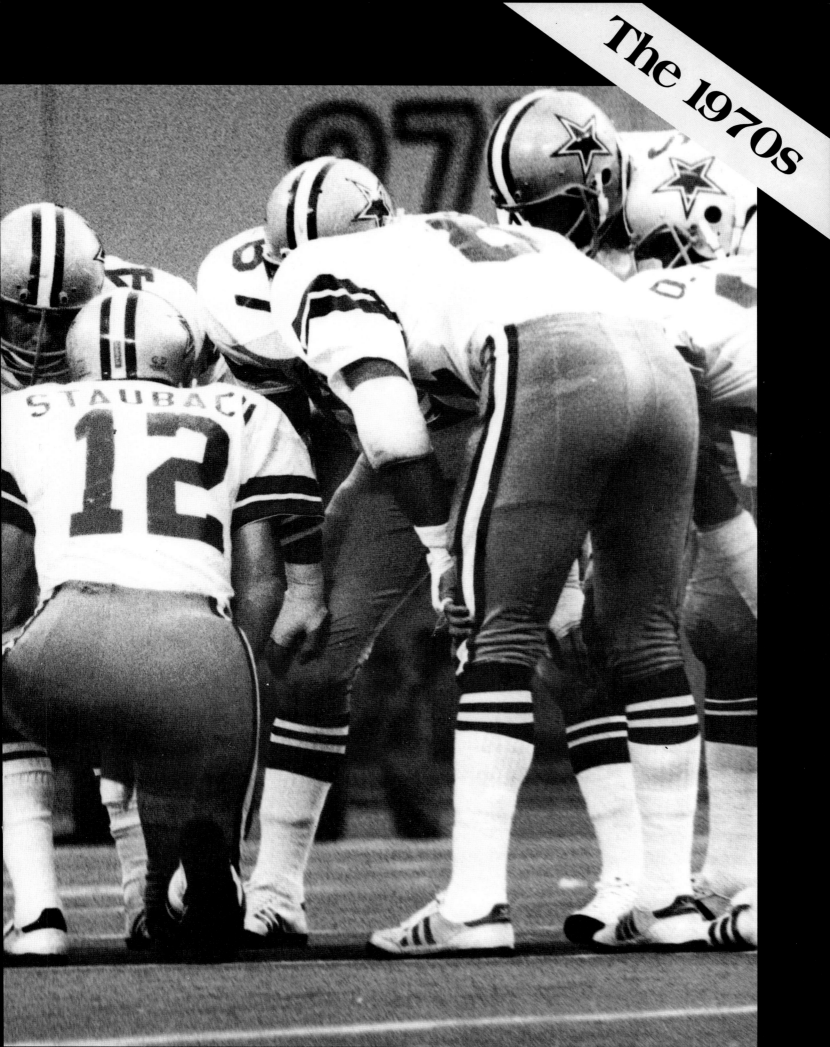

Compared to the sixties, with its war with the AFL, and the eighties, with its off-field battles, the seventies for the NFL were truly a time of peace and tranquility.

Sure, there was still another new kid on the block – the World Football League. But with the exception of driving players' salaries toward the ionosphere, the WFL was more an amusement than a threat. The WFL did gain some notoriety when it signed members of the Dolphins' Super Bowl team to future contracts – much like what Al Davis did in the last days of the AFL. Gary Davidson was the force behind the WFL. Similar brain children of this entrepreneur were the American Basketball Association and the World Hockey League.

When the Miami Three – Larry Csonka, Jim Kiick and Paul Warfield – finally arrived in the WFL (1975), their team, the Memphis Southmen or Grizzlies (take your pick), like others in the ill-conceived league, would play just a little more than half a season. The WFL would fold amid some of the more bizarre incidents associated with any sports league.

The Dolphins under Don Shula became pro football's second modern-day dynasty, achieving three straight Super Bowl appearances – two of them resulting in victory – and perfection with a 17-0 record in 1972. The Dallas Cowboys – a team that Texas would have to share with the rest of America – were somewhat dynastic themselves. They were in five Super Bowls during the decade, winning two.

But the real dynasty of the seventies was lurking just below the horizon.

In 42 years in the NFL, Art Rooney and his Steelers had won nothing in the way of championships. Chuck Noll took over coaching duties in 1969 and immediately won the season's opener – then lost the next 13 games of the year. Cries of SOS, "Same Old Steelers," echoed through Western Pennsylvania. But Noll, working through the draft, soon turned out the Team of the Seventies. The Steelers would lay waste to the rest of the NFL once they started winning. After their first divi-

sional title in 1972 gave them a taste of glory, Rooney's "lovable losers" turned into 47 Atilla the Huns – pillaging and plundering, some would say, their way to four Super Bowl titles in a six-year span. Chuck Noll never lost in four Super Bowl appearances. No other coach could make that claim.

There were labor disputes in 1970 and 1974, but they were settled in the preseason – no real harm done, except maybe to give a larger number of rookies jobs at the expense of some veterans.

Monday, September 21, 1970, isn't a date as infamous as December 7, 1941, but it is noteworthy just the same. It was the first Monday Night Football broadcast carried nationally in prime time by ABC. The Browns defeated the Jets 31-21 in a rather ordinary game, but the telecast was anything but ordinary. Howard Cosell – vocabulary, opinions, misinformation and all – was thrust upon an unsuspecting nation. Monday Night Football, with Cosell, Don Meredith and Frank Gifford, became a cult within a cult. It changed the viewing habits of men *and* women, not to mention the nation's sleeping habits. For many years, CBS and NBC tried unsuccessfully to lure viewers away from the ritualistic telecasts. At first thought to be an anticlimax to the football weekend, Monday Night Football soon proved to be the crescendo toward which the NFL's weekend activities built. If pro football was ready to celebrate a widespread and fanatical following, Monday Night Football in the seventies was a big reason for it.

Couch potatoes throughout the land propped themselves up on one elbow and applauded George Blanda in 1970. On five successive weeks, the 43-year-old quarterback/kicker prevented what seemed to be sure defeat for the Raiders, often in the final moments of the game.

Expansion came to the NFL in 1976 with the advent of the Seattle Seahawks and Tampa Bay Buccaneers. Seattle became somewhat respectable in its infancy, but Tampa Bay – under John McKay – set an all-time record for futility by losing its first 26 games. McKay, ever the

DECADE STANDINGS – 1970s National Football Conference		
Team	W-L-T	Percentage
Dallas Cowboys[1]	105-39-0	.729
Minnesota Vikings[2]	99-43-2	.694
Los Angeles Rams[3]	98-42-4	.694
Washington Redskins[4]	91-52-1	.635
St. Louis Cardinals	69-71-4	.493
Detroit Lions	66-75-3	.469
Atlanta Falcons	60-81-3	.427
San Francisco 49ers	60-82-4	.424
Chicago Bears	60-83-1	.420
Green Bay Packers	57-82-5	.413
Philadelphia Eagles	56-84-4	.403
New York Giants	50-93-1	.351
New Orleans Saints	42-98-4	.306
Tampa Bay Buccaneers	17-43-0	.283

[1]*won NFC titles in 1970, 1971, 1975, 1977 and 1978; won SB VI and SB XII.*
[2]*won NFC titles in 1973, 1974 and 1976.*
[3]*won NFC title in 1979.*
[4]*won NFC title in 1972.*

Pages 132-133: *With Jack Ham (59) looking over their shoulders, the Dallas Cowboys – the NFL's winningest team of the seventies – and Roger Staubach (12) huddle.*

Opposite above: *The Dallas Cowboys' cheerleaders combine glamor and enthusiasm.*

Opposite below: *"The Prez" to some, "the Chief" to others, Art Rooney was the most revered figure in the NFL until his death in 1988. Fortunately, he lived long enough to see his Pittsburgh Steelers shake their lovable-losers tag and win four Super Bowls. What he did for the NFL is well-documented. What he did behind the scenes for his fellow man may never be fully known.*

quipster, when asked what he thought of his team's execution, said "I'm in favor of it."

Playing facilities also experienced expansion. A dozen teams moved into different ballparks – 11 of them going into newly-constructed stadiums. The Steelers and Bengals began play in 1970 in Three Rivers and Riverfront, respectively. In 1971 the Patriots, Cowboys and Eagles opened Schaefer, Texas and Veterans stadiums, respectively. The Chiefs and Arrowhead were paired in 1972. The Bills opened Rich Stadium the next year. The Saints moved into the long-awaited Louisiana Superdome in 1975, and the Lions began play in Pontiac's Silverdome that year also. Giants Stadium opened in 1976, as did Seattle's Kingdome. For good measure, the Bears moved fields from Wrigley to Soldier and the 49ers left venerated Kezar for Candlestick Park.

DECADE STANDINGS – 1970s
American Football Conference

Team	W-L-T	Percentage
Miami Dolphins[1]	104-39-1	.726
Oakland Raiders[2]	100-38-6	.715
Pittsburgh Steelers[3]	99-44-1	.691
Denver Broncos[4]	75-64-5	.538
Cincinnati Bengals	74-70-0	.514
Baltimore Colts[5]	73-70-1	.510
Cleveland Browns	72-70-2	.507
Boston/New England Patriots	66-78-0	.458
Kansas City Chiefs	60-79-5	.434
Houston Oilers	60-82-2	.424
San Diego Chargers	58-81-5	.420
Seattle Seahawks	25-35-0	.417
New York Jets	53-91-0	.368
Buffalo Bills	51-91-2	.361

[1] won AFC titles in 1971, 1972 and 1973; won SB VII and SB VIII.
[2] won AFC title in 1976; won SB XI.
[3] won AFC titles in 1974, 1975, 1978 and 1979; won SB IX, SB X, SB XIII and SB XIV.
[4] won AFC title in 1977.
[5] won AFC title in 1970; won SB V.

ROGER THE DODGER, SNAKE, SHACK AND OTHERS
Quarterbacks

Top Rushing Quarterbacks of All Time			
Player	Attempts	Yards	Average	Touchdowns
Randall Cunningham	573	3,986	7.0	28
Fran Tarkenton	675	3,674	5.4	32
Tobin Rote	635	3,068	4.8	35
Greg Landry	439	2,655	6.2	21
Bobby Douglass	410	2,654	6.5	22
Bobby Layne	611	2,451	4.0	25
Roger Staubach	410	2,264	5.5	20
Terry Bradshaw	444	2,257	5.1	32

Opposite: *James Harris, called "Shack" for a never-disclosed reason, was another Grambling graduate. He was the first black NFL quarterback to start over a sustained period. After being released by the Bills in 1972, Harris went on to be very productive – NFC passing leader, 1976 – with the L.A. Rams.*

Above: *Ken "Snake" Stabler (12) had the look and the mindset of an Old West gunslinger. He was the master of the Oakland Raiders' vertical passing game, and most dangerous with time running out.*

Left: *Bert Jones was the class of NFL quarterbacks in his prime with the Baltimore Colts during the mid-seventies.*

Page 138: *Archie Manning (8), called "the greatest college quarterback ever" by no less an authority than Beau Riffenburgh, could have sued his New Orleans Saints teammates for non-support.*

Page 139: *Roger Staubach of the Dallas Cowboys became a legend despite his navy obligation delaying his NFL debut by several seasons.*

FLYING FEET AND VELCRO FINGERS
Receivers

**A Comparison of NFL Receivers of the 1970s by Number of Receptions,
Yardage Gained, and Average Per Catch**

No. of Receptions	Yardage Gained	Average per catch
1. Harold Jackson – 432	Harold Jackson – 7,724	Mel Gray – 20.0
2. Harold Carmichael – 407	Ken Burrough – 6,343	Paul Warfield – 19.9
3. Bob Tucker – 407	Gene Washington (SF) – 6,145	John Gilliam – 19.4
4. Ken Burrough – 377	Haven Moses – 5,786	Gary Garrison – 18.9
5. Lydell Mitchell – 374	Drew Pearson – 5,713	Haven Moses – 18.4

Opposite above: *Yes, Virginia, there were two Gene Washingtons in the NFL at the same time. Both were talented wide receivers, shown here at the 1971 Pro Bowl. Gene Washington (L) of the Minnesota Vikings was from the fine Michigan State teams of the mid-sixties. Gene Washington (R) of the San Francisco 49ers was from Stanford, where he played quarterback before concentrating on being a wideout. Michigan State's Gene won three Big 10 hurdles championships and one NCAA title. A No. 1 draft choice in 1967, he caught only 13 passes as a rookie, but for a 29.5-yard average. He ended his career with the Broncos in 1973. Stanford's Gene came into the league in 1969 and promptly went to four consecutive Pro Bowls. During his career with the 49ers, and a final season (1979) with the Lions, he caught 385 passes for 6,856 yards and 60 touchdowns.*

Opposite below: *Ken Burrough (00) of the Houston Oilers catches the game-winning TD in a 1979 battle with the Cowboys. Burrough was a big (6′ 3″, 210 lbs.) rookie with the Saints in 1970 and caught 13 passes. Short-sightedly, they traded him to Houston the next year, where he went on to have a most productive career. Twice a year – and sometimes again in the playoffs – Burrough would line up against a former college cornerback opponent, Mel Blount of the Steelers. After a decade of this, a writer asked Burrough if he knew Blount. Double Zero replied, "I played against him four years in college. I played against him at least twice a year in the pros for 10 or 11 seasons. Yeah, I know Mel Blount – better than my wife." Burrough retired after the 1981 season with 421 catches for 7,102 yards and 49 touchdowns.*

Right: *Ahmad Rashad came into the NFL in 1972 as Bobby Moore. He had been a running back at Oregon, but quickly changed his name and position. With the Bills and later with the Minnesota Vikings, Rashad developed into one of the game's premier receivers. Here he has just out-wrestled Bengals cornerback Ken Riley, a vastly underrated player, for the ball. Rashad is now one of the better ex-player broadcasters on network TV.*

Left above: *Harold Carmichael (17) of the Philadelphia Eagles, at 6' 7", was one of the tallest receivers to play the game. From 1971 to 1984, he was also one of the best. Early in his NFL career, he was hampered by his team's lack of a top level quarterback. That changed with Roman Gabriel. Later it was Ron Jaworski. In 1973 Carmichael led the NFL with 67 catches for 1,116 yards. He played in his first Pro Bowl after that season. Carmichael established a record for the most consecutive games with at least one reception – 127 games (1972-80). The record has since been broken by Steve Largent (177) and Ozzie Newsome (150).*

Left below: *For someone who started out as a quarterback – at South River High (New Jersey) right after Joe Theismann – and a free agent from the University of Tulsa, Drew Pearson made a real impact on the NFL, 1973-83. He may be best remembered for hauling in Roger Staubach's "Hail Mary" pass late in the 1975 playoff game that crushed the Vikings' hopes of going to the Super Bowl. Minnesotans contend that Pearson pushed off of Nate Wright to take the winning 50-yarder, but a look at the game film shows no such evidence.*

Opposite and Inset: *Paul Warfield (42) came into the NFL in 1964 with a handicap. He played college football at Ohio State in Woody Hayes's "three yards and a cloud of dust" offense. When he said goodbye to Columbus, Warfield had only 39 receptions to his credit, and was used more as a runner than receiver. This didn't stop the Cleveland Browns from projecting him as a wide receiver. In his career with the Browns and Dolphins, Warfield caught only 427 passes, compared to Steve Largent's 819. But Warfield was always there for the clutch catch and his average gain was high. And no wideout ever blocked better than the smooth and fluid Warfield. As classy a person as he was a player, Warfield is in the Hall of Fame.*

THE UNCONQUERED
The Perfect '72 Dolphins

Left: *In 1972 the Miami Dolphins did what no other NFL team had done before or since. They won every regular season game, each playoff, and the Super Bowl. That made them 17-0. And they did it the hard way. Early in the season, starting quarterback Bob Griese went down with an ankle injury. Not to worry. Coach Don Shula (center, between Howard Twilley and Griese) had reliable backup Earl Morrall. Morrall sustained the team through the season and into the early playoff rounds until Griese returned. Helping Morrall shoulder the load was a punishing ground game and the emerging "No Name Defense."*

Opposite and Inset: *Key to the infantry attack was fullback Larry Csonka (39). Zonk was big (6' 3", 237 lbs.), if somewhat slower than the ideal running back, and when he came to the Dolphins there was talk of making him a linebacker. Cooler heads prevailed, and the ex-Syracuse Orangeman became the NFL's premier power runner. No one was more reliable on "third and short" than Csonka. He ran low to the ground, never lifting his feet very high. This gave him great balance to go along with his size and power. Game film from Super Bowl VII, which the Dolphins won from the Redskins, 14-7, shows him flicking off some would-be tacklers and giving others a free ride. Just as it was said of Jim Brown in his prime: "the lucky ones fell off." Csonka had a great forward lean, which meant he was never knocked backwards when being tackled, which in turn meant two extra yards each time he carried the ball. Also sharing the running responsibilities were Jim Kiick – "Butch Cassidy" to Zonk's "Sundance Kid" – and Eugene "Mercury" Morris. It was during the 1972 season that Csonka (1,117 yards) and Morris (an even 1,000) became the first two NFL runners from the same backfield to each gain a thousand yards in the same year. Kiick's contribution was more as a third-down specialist, adept at catching passes and running.*

Left and Below: *Griese (12) was never more Griese than he was in Super Bowl VII. The ex-Purdue All-America threw only 11 passes, but completed 8 for 88 yards and a touchdown – a 28-yarder to Twilley for the game's first score. He directed the ground game (Csonka 115 yards, Kiick 38, and Morris 34) flawlessly. By controlling the ball on offense, the No Names – featuring Vern Den Herder, Manny Fernandez, Bob Heinz, Bill Stanfill, Doug Swift, Nick Buoniconti, Mike Kolen, Lloyd Mumphord, Curtis Johnson, Dick Anderson and Jake Scott – were well-rested.*

Opposite: *In Super Bowl VII action, Mercury Morris (22) gains big yardage. It's been said that SB VII was the most lopsided 14-7 game ever. Miami was in control all the way.*

MEN OF STEEL
Steelers of the Seventies

The 1975 Pittsburgh Steelers' Defensive Statistics Contrasted with Leading Teams of Other Decades
Figures in ( ) represent per-game average, since teams played varying numbers of games per season.

	STEELERS	'48 Eagles	'56 Giants	'62 Packers	'85 Bears	'90 Giants
First Downs	214 (15.28)	158 (13.16)★	188 (15.66)	191 (13.64)	236 (14.75)	245 (15.31)
By Rushing	91 (6.50)	62 (5.16)	82 (6.83)	88 (6.28)	74 (4.62)★	90 (5.62)
By Passing	97 (6.92)	83 (6.91)★	90 (7.50)	94 (6.71)	141 (8.81)	139 (8.68)
By Penalty	26 (1.85)	13 (1.08)	16 (1.33)	9 (0.64)★	21 (1.31)	16 (1.00)
Total Yards	3,361 (261.50)	3,169 (264.08)	3,081 (256.75)	3,277 (234.07)★	4,135 (258.43)	4,206 (262.83)
Rushing	1,825 (130.35)	1,209 (100.75)	1,443 (120.25)	1,531 (109.35)	1,319 (82.43)★	1,459 (91.18)
Passing	2,194 (156.71)	1,951 (162.58)	1,638 (136.50)	1,746 (124.71)★	3,299 (206.18)	2,933 (183.31)
Average Gain Per Rush	4.2	3.2★	3.5	3.8	3.7	3.8
Pass Completion %	46.2	41.1★	50.2	52.7	47.7	56.0
Average Gain Per Play	4.2★	4.3	4.3	4.3	4.4	4.6
Opponents' Points	162 (11.57)	156 (13.00)	197 (16.41)	148 (10.57)★	198 (12.37)	211 (13.18)
Touchdowns	19 (1.35)	22 (1.83)	25 (2.08)	17 (1.21)★	23 (1.43)	23 (1.43)
By Rushing	8 (0.57)	5 (0.41)	11 (0.91)	4 (0.28)★	6 (0.37)	9 (0.56)
By Passing	9 (0.64)★	14 (1.16)	12 (1.00)	10 (0.71)	16 (1.00)	12 (0.75)

★leader in category.

Opposite: *Chuck Noll, architect of the Pittsburgh Steelers' four Super Bowl victories, was often depicted as tight-lipped. Here, after Franco Harris's "Immaculate Reception" against the Raiders in 1972, Noll proved he could smile.*

Right: *Lynn Swann (88) and John Stallworth (82) may not have been as funny as Laurel & Hardy, especially to cornerbacks, but they were a deadly duo when it came to catching the football.*

Below: *Rocky Bleier's story has been well-documented in the book and movie* Fighting Back. *Wounded in Vietnam, he came back by sheer will to be a valued team member. He worked diligently in the weight room and was faster after his injuries than before. His blocking was so devastating he was called "the third guard."*

Below right: *Terry Bradshaw came out of little Louisiana Tech in 1970. He struggled early, but matured into one of the best. A superb athlete, Bradshaw once held the national high school javelin record.*

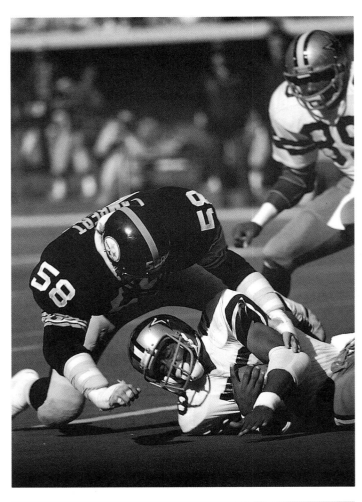

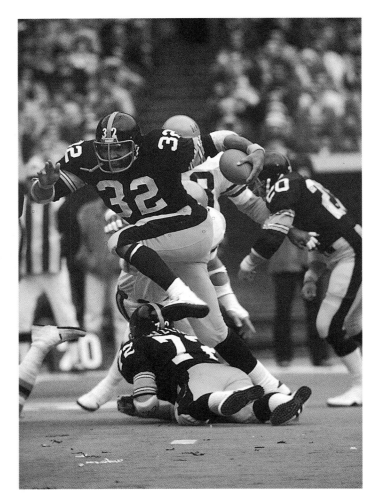

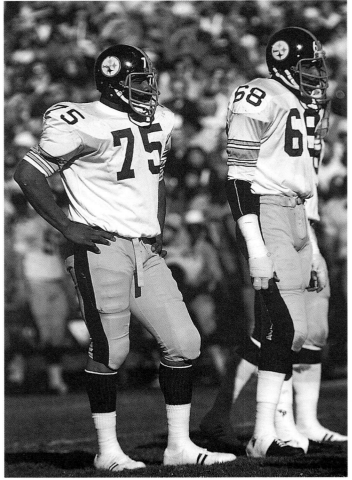

Opposite above left: *Jack Lambert (58), enveloping Tony Dorsett, came to the Pittsburgh Steelers as a skinny (6' 5", 214 lbs.) defensive end from Kent State. He immediately became the blood and guts of the Steel Curtain defense as its leader/middle linebacker.*

Opposite above right: *Franco Harris (32) was overshadowed at Penn State by teammate Lydell Mitchell. But as a rookie in 1972 he had his moments in the sun, and would continue to shine for years to come. Franco was at his best when an important game was on the line. His 1,556 yards rushing in post-season play are, by far, the most in NFL history. Harris's 12,120 career rushing yards (post-season totals excluded) are fifth-best ever. Assisting Franco in this 1975 game against the Bengals are Bleier (20) and Gerry "Moon" Mullins (72).*

Opposite below left: *Joe Greene (75) and L. C. Greenwood both joined the Steelers in 1969. Greene was an immediate star (Rookie of the Year); Greenwood took a while to develop. At their peak – along with Dwight White, Ernie Holmes, Steve Furness, and John Banaszak – they formed the Steel Curtain, and no one had an easy time getting by them. Greene could, and sometimes did, shoulder the responsibility of a Steelers' victory by himself. Greenwood was a demon pass-rusher. In Super Bowl IX, like an NBA center, the 6' 6" Greenwood "rejected" a considerable number of Fran Tarkenton's passes.*

Opposite below right: *Mike Webster – part of the '74 draft that brought Swann, Lambert and Stallworth to the team – replaced ironman Ray Mansfield (182 games at center) and became an ironman himself (220 games – most in team history). Webster lived in the weight room, where he, Jon Kolb, Jim Clack and Rocky Bleier could pump 550 pounds of iron in the benchpress.*

Right: *Floyd Little finds out what many others did: it's hard to escape Jack Ham (59). Now that Lawrence Taylor has proved human, Ham is still the template for linebackers.*

SOME OF THE BEST
Great Super Bowls of the Seventies

Left: *The Dallas Cowboys and Pittsburgh Steelers could always be trusted to produce an exciting Super Bowl. Lynn Swann (88, stepping away from Mark Washington en route to a fourth-quarter TD) provided the pyrotechnics in SB X. He caught 4 passes for 161 yards and MVP honors. The Steelers won, 21-17.*

Below: *In Super Bowl XIII Franco Harris (32) scores on a big play – a 22-yard touchdown run, right up the middle – in a big game. As he was about to erupt, Harris would get "that look" in his eyes. Right before this play, Franco had it. The score was a key in the Steelers' 35-31 triumph over the Cowboys.*

Opposite: *Jim O'Brien was a rookie wide receiver/kicker with the Baltimore Colts when they went to Super Bowl V. With the game on the line and five seconds to play, O'Brien connected from the 32-yard line to lift his team over the Cowboys, 16-13. Earl Morrall gave the first-year kicker a perfect spot and hold.*

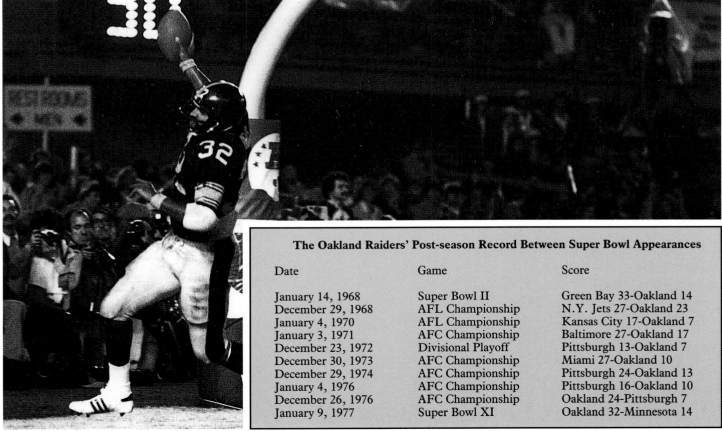

The Oakland Raiders' Post-season Record Between Super Bowl Appearances

Date	Game	Score
January 14, 1968	Super Bowl II	Green Bay 33-Oakland 14
December 29, 1968	AFL Championship	N.Y. Jets 27-Oakland 23
January 4, 1970	AFL Championship	Kansas City 17-Oakland 7
January 3, 1971	AFC Championship	Baltimore 27-Oakland 17
December 23, 1972	Divisional Playoff	Pittsburgh 13-Oakland 7
December 30, 1973	AFC Championship	Miami 27-Oakland 10
December 29, 1974	AFC Championship	Pittsburgh 24-Oakland 13
January 4, 1976	AFC Championship	Pittsburgh 16-Oakland 10
December 26, 1976	AFC Championship	Oakland 24-Pittsburgh 7
January 9, 1977	Super Bowl XI	Oakland 32-Minnesota 14

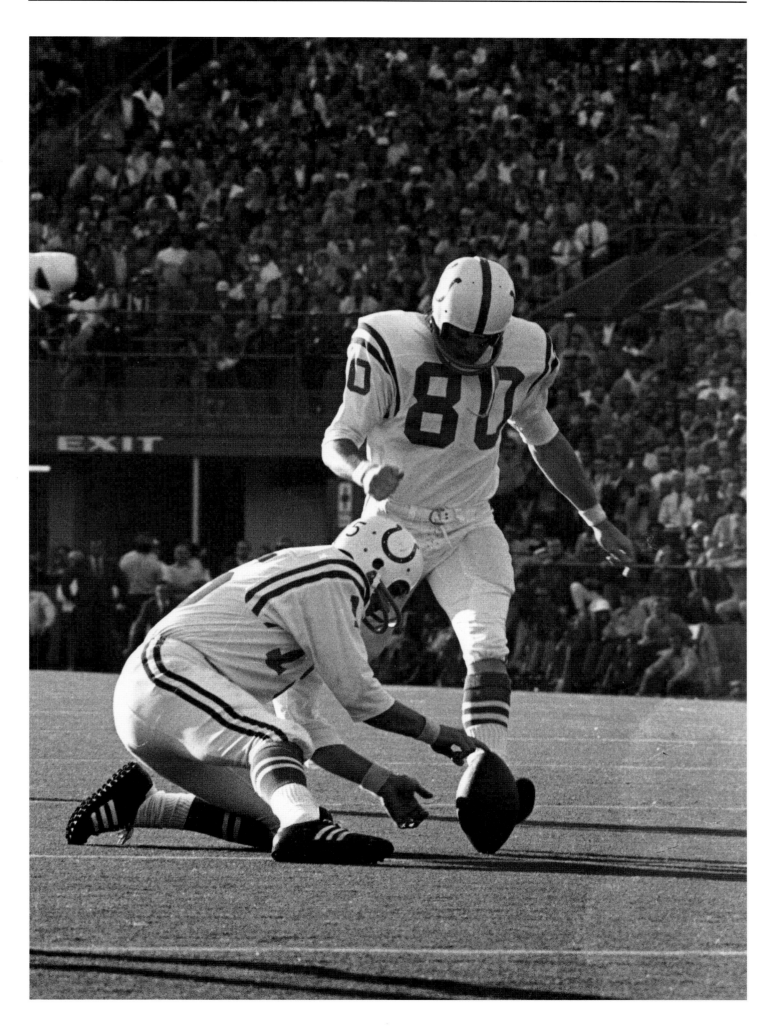

Left above: *Two of the keys to the Cowboys' five Super Bowl appearances – Tom Landry (left) and Roger Staubach – confer during SB XIII.*

Left: *Just as Jim O'Brien (80) lifted his team to victory in Super Bowl V, his team did the same for him. Giving the young kicker a boost are Tom Nowatzke (34), taxi-squadder Lynn Larson, and Earl Morrall (15).*

Above: *Too Tall is too much! In Super Bowl XII, Ed "Too Tall" Jones (6' 9", 265 lbs.) unloads on hapless Broncos quarterback Craig Morton (7). The Cowboys completely shut down Denver's attack, winning 27-10. So dominant was Dallas's defense that the co-Most Valuable Players for the game were defensive end Harvey Martin and defensive tackle Randy White.*

Opposite: *Roger Staubach was very sharp in Super Bowl XII – 17 of 25 for 183 yards and a touchdown. Morton was 4 of 15 for 39 yards and 4 interceptions. Oddly, Staubach and Morton had competed for the starting job when both were with Dallas.*

RUNNIN' WILD
Great Running Backs

**The 10 Leading Rushers of 1976 Contrasted with the
10 Runners with the Best Per-Carry Average Gain**

YARDS		AVERAGE*	
1. O.J. Simpson	1,503	Don Calhoun	5.58
2. Walter Payton	1,390	O.J. Simpson	5.18
3. Delvin Williams	1,203	Rickey Young	4.95
4. Lydell Mitchell	1,200	Delvin Williams	4.85
5. Lawrence McCutcheon	1,168	Sam Cunningham	4.79
6. Chuck Foreman	1,155	Gregg Pruitt	4.78
7. Franco Harris	1,128	Rocky Bleier	4.71
8. Mike Thomas	1,101	Clark Gaines	4.61
9. Rocky Bleier	1,036	Mike Hogan	4.56
10. Mark van Eeghen	1,012	Sherman Smith	4.51

minimum 100 carries

Opposite: *O. J. Simpson (32) – shown here in 1973, the year he would gain 2,003 yards – was the first to crack 2,000 yards. Oddly enough, the USC Heisman Trophy winner was used as a decoy when he first joined the Buffalo Bills. Then Lou Saban came along, and a great offensive line – The Electric Company, they turned on the Juice – followed.*

Right: *Calvin Hill (35) joined the Dallas Cowboys right off the Yale campus in 1969. He earned Rookie of the Year honors with 942 rushing yards and went on to gain a thousand yards, or close to it, several more times.*

Below: *Earl Campbell (34) was truly a force with the Houston Oilers. Said Bum Phillips, "If he ain't in a class by himself, it don't take long to call roll."*

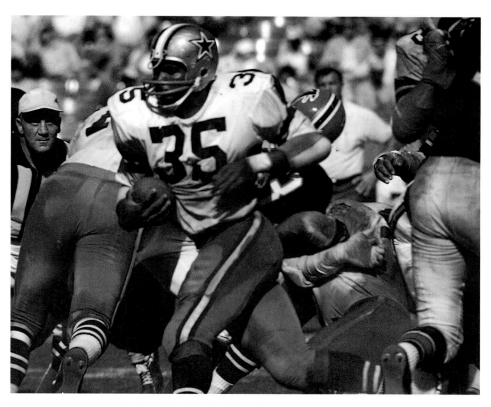

Opposite: *Tony Dorsett (33) is about to elude the Redskins' Perry Brooks (69) in this 1981 game. Going back to his days at Hopewell High in the Western Pennsylvania milltown of Aliquippa, through a Heisman Trophy-winning career at Pitt, and on to the Dallas Cowboys, Dorsett would gain more than 1,000 yards annually until the 1982 players' strike shortened the NFL season to just nine regular season games. This covered a span of 14 years. Dorsett, called "Hawkeye" because of his larger-than-average eyes, had excellent field vision to go with his speed. While he appeared somewhat small at 5' 11", 190 pounds, a trip to the Cowboys' locker room would reveal a muscular torso that looked as if it were carved out of ebony. Dorsett's speed was "as fast as it needed to be." Once in a Monday Night Football game against the Vikings, with the ball on the Cowboys' own one-yard line, Dorsett not only avoided the safety, but everything else. Ninety-nine yards later, he was the sole owner of the NFL record for the longest run from scrimmage.*

Right: *Jim Otis (35, white jersey), is a textbook example of an over-achiever. Generously listed as 6' 0", he was not very fast, either. He simply did his damnedest! That's what Woody Hayes liked in his fullbacks at Ohio State. Otis was a consensus All-America for the Buckeyes and Big-10 MVP as a senior in 1969. Drafted by the Saints in the ninth round, he played little as a rookie and was traded to the Chiefs. He did even less there – because he wasn't given the chance – and was then waived. In 1973 the St. Louis Cardinals paid the $100 waiver price and never regretted it. In 1975 Otis banged and bounced his way to 1,076 yards – more than any other NFC runner. Here, Otis is barging into the end zone on a one-yard plunge against the Giants. Not only did he score, he broke Johnny Roland's team career rushing record of 3,608 yards. Otis powers past Ernie Jones (35), George Martin (on the ground), and Harry Carson (right).*

BRIDESMAIDS
Vikings – Good Team Loses Four Super Bowls

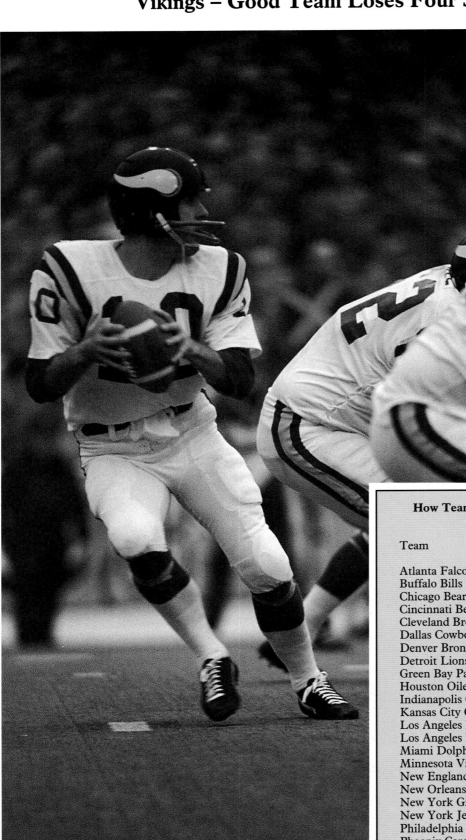

Left: *The Minnesota Vikings were a good team under coach Bud Grant, but they have not escaped the stigma of coming up short in the only four Super Bowls in which they have played. They lost SB IV, SB VIII, SB IX, and SB XI. The quarterback in three of those games was Fran Tarkenton (10).*

Opposite: *Helping to get the Vikings to those Super Bowls was a defensive unit called "the Purple People Eaters" (after a fifties novelty tune). Offensively, it is doubtful if a better all-around back than Chuck Foreman (44) existed. He's seen here in Super Bowl XI action, being hemmed in by Willie Hall (39), Otis Sistrunk (60) – described by Alex Karras as being "from the University of Mars" – and Ted Hendricks (83). Referee Lou Palazzi checks for infractions. Perhaps Foreman's best year was 1975 when he narrowly missed a "triple crown" – rushing for 1,070 yards (second in the NFC), 73 receptions (first in the NFL), and 22 touchdowns (second in the NFL).*

How Teams First Qualified for Post-season Playoffs Under the New Format of 1970

Team	Year/Qualifier
Atlanta Falcons	1980 – NFC West
Buffalo Bills	1980 – AFC East
Chicago Bears	1984 – NFC Central
Cincinnati Bengals	1970 – AFC Central
Cleveland Browns	1971 – AFC Central
Dallas Cowboys	1970 – NFC East
Denver Broncos	1977 – AFC West
Detroit Lions	1970 – NFC Wildcard
Green Bay Packers	1972 – NFC Central
Houston Oilers	1978 – AFC Wildcard
Indianapolis Colts	1970 – AFC East (as Baltimore)
Kansas City Chiefs	1971 – AFC West
Los Angeles Raiders	1970 – AFC West (as Oakland)
Los Angeles Rams	1973 – NFC West
Miami Dolphins	1970 – AFC Wildcard
Minnesota Vikings	1970 – NFC Central
New England Patriots	1978 – AFC East
New Orleans Saints	1987 – NFC Wildcard
New York Giants	1984 – NFC Wildcard
New York Jets	1981 – AFC Wildcard
Philadelphia Eagles	1979 – NFC Wildcard
Phoenix Cardinals	1974 – NFC East (as St. Louis)
Pittsburgh Steelers	1972 – AFC Central
San Diego Chargers	1979 – AFC West
San Francisco 49ers	1970 – NFC West
Seattle Seahawks	1984 – AFC Wildcard
Tampa Bay Buccaneers	1979 – NFC Central
Washington Redskins	1971 – NFC Wildcard

UNDERAPPRECIATED

Opposite: *For various reasons, some very good players get overlooked. None more so than the San Francisco 49ers' Dave Wilcox (64). In his 11-year career (1964-74), he made the Pro Bowl seven times. Wilcox, out of Oregon, was said to have had "long arms and sharp elbows." Quarterback Pete Liske (14) of the Eagles can at least attest to the long arms.*

Right: *Tommy Nobis (60) had the misfortune of being a good player (several times All-Pro) on a bad team (the Atlanta Falcons). Nevertheless, he was appreciated by his peers. Many opponents, speaking from experience, have said, "Nobody hit harder than Nobis." Chronic knee problems curtailed his effectiveness.*

Below: *To say a Hall of Famer is underappreciated is a contradiction in terms, but Ken Houston (27) never got his due with the Houston Oilers or Washington Redskins.*

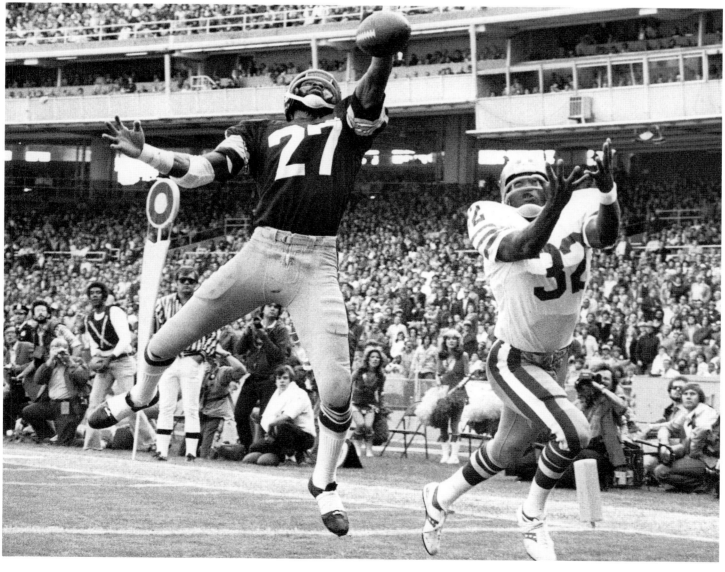

BRILLIANT BACKERS

Opposite: *Chuck Howley (54) of the Dallas Cowboys, making one of his two interceptions in Super Bowl V, was the first non-quarterback to win Super Bowl MVP honors, and is still the only one to be chosen from a losing team, as the Cowboys lost to the Colts, 16-13. After two seasons with the Bears, Howley was traded to Dallas in 1961.*

Above: *No one intimidated better than the Chicago Bears' Dick Butkus (51). Here he tackles the Patriots' Sam "Bam" Cunningham (39).*

Right: *If, and it's a big if, anyone was more of an intimidator than Butkus, it was the Green Bay Packers' Ray Nitschke (66). For 15 seasons, this Hall of Famer helped the Black & Blue Division (NFC-Central) earn its nickname.*

Page 166: *Butkus, football's version of "the Terminator," is telling a Broncos runner – "You come this way again, you'll get more of the same." Fellow linebacker Doug Buffone (55) looks on, as an official takes the ball.*

Page 167 with Inset: *Mike Curtis (32) was called "the Animal." He once decked a fan who ran onto the field to steal the game ball. Curtis was a fine fullback/linebacker at Duke before joining the Colts in Baltimore. He was at his best as an outside linebacker. After moving to the middle, a teammate said, "Mike was more interested in beating up on the offensive guards" – ignoring runners. Still, he was very effective wherever he was.*

FOOTBALLS FOR FOOTLIGHTS
Players Who Went into Acting

Opposite: *Since pro football is entertainment, it's only natural some players succumb to the "smell of the greasepaint and the roar of the crowd." Alex Karras, who got his start playing himself in* Paper Lion, *was cast as Mongo in* Blazing Saddles.

Above: *O. J. Simpson debuted in 1974 in the Paramount Pictures' release,* The Klansman. *Lee Marvin (right), as a sheriff, seems to be giving Simpson, a member of a gang, the opportunity to change his ways – or else.*

Right: *Joe Namath was appropriately cast in* The Last Rebel. *It was Namath's third feature film, and was shot overseas in Rome.*

Left above: *Dating back to 1926, when Red Grange starred in* One Minute to Play, *pro football players have gone to Hollywood. Will Walls, a New York Giants end at the time, had a minor role in the wartime epic* Thirty Seconds Over Tokyo. *Bob Waterfield began as a stuntman while still at UCLA. After his marriage to Jane Russell, he moved to on-camera roles in several 1950s films. The entire Rams team was featured in some films, and their game-film footage was often used in Hollywood football films. Mike Henry, a Steelers linebacker from USC in the sixties, was traded at his request to the Rams so he could be the latest "Tarzan." As pro football became more accepted, more players got major roles. One of the first to star was Jim Brown, here with Raquel Welch in* 100 Rifles.

Left below: *Ed Marinaro, after setting Ivy League and NCAA records at Cornell, was a better-than-average running back with the Vikings and Jets. Never seriously interested in acting during his NFL career, he quickly broke in after his playing days. As Sgt. Joe Coffey, he had a featured role in the critically-acclaimed TV series "Hill Street Blues."*

Opposite: *Perhaps no actor/athlete ever enjoyed the credibility and acceptance that Merlin Olsen did, and does. Whether in a TV or movie role, as a network commentator, or as a spokesman for a product, Olsen exhibits a rare form of trustworthiness. Olsen, an Academic All-America at Utah State, began with bit parts early in his Rams career. He soon graduated to bigger roles and was featured as Jonathan Garvey on "Little House on the Prairie." Later, he had his own show: "Father Murphy." As a player, Olsen was subjected to the questionable tactics of Cardinals guard Conrad Dobler. Olsen retaliated, after a fashion, by having Dobler's name placed on a tombstone in a scene in one TV episode. As a color commentator, Olsen was less flashy than John Madden, but he was a favorite of knowledgeable fans.*

FOND FAREWELLS

Opposite: *Larry Wilson of the St. Louis Cardinals, pioneer of the safety blitz, was called, "pound-for-pound, the toughest player in the game." He once intercepted a pass with his elbows, literally, as he played with two broken hands in plaster casts. Wilson retired in 1973.*

Right: *Cincinnati Bengals tackle Mike Reid retired at the peak of his All-Pro career in 1974 and pursued a career in music.*

Below: *How good was Merlin Olsen with the L.A. Rams? He made 14 Pro Bowls in a 15-year career.*

Below right: *Weeb Ewbank, a head coach from 1954 to 1973, is the only man to win World Championships in both the NFL and the AFL.*

DECADE HIGHLIGHTS

Left: *One of the storied moments in pro football history was Franco Harris's "Immaculate Reception." It enabled the Pittsburgh Steelers to win their first-ever post-season game, in 1972. On a desperation fourth-down attempt, Franco plucked a ricocheted Terry Bradshaw pass off his shoetops and romped 60 yards to score. The Raiders claimed the play was illegal – being tipped from Steeler to Steeler. But the officials agreed that Jack Tatum of the Raiders tipped the ball, and it was Pittsburgh 13-Oakland 7.*

Below: *When no one else wanted to, ABC took a chance on "Monday Night Football." During the seventies, (left to right) Don Meredith, Howard Cosell and Frank Gifford were like "weekly visitors."*

Opposite above: *Tom Dempsey of the New Orleans Saints (dark jersey) overcame physical handicaps – note right arm and foot – to become an NFL kicker. His 63-yarder ended this game in 1970 in the final seconds, and set a still-standing NFL record.*

Opposite below: *Russ Francis (81) of the New England Patriots was a do-everything tight end, and termed "All-World" by Cosell.*

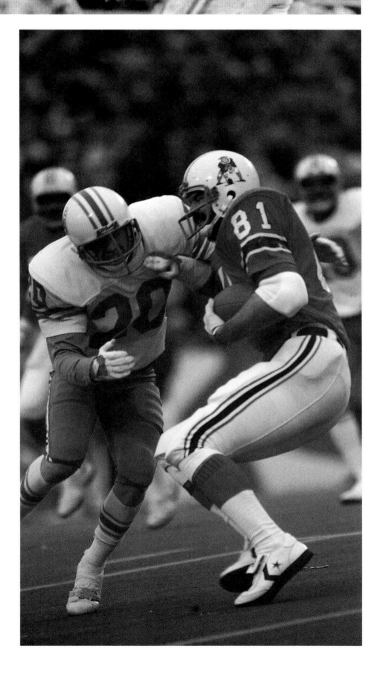

DECADE LEADERS, 1970s – NFC	
PASSING	
Yardage: Fran Tarkenton	23,863
Completion Percentage: Fran Tarkenton	59.7%
Touchdowns: Fran Tarkenton	156
RUSHING	
Yardage: Walter Payton	6,926
Per Carry Average: Tony Dorsett	4.6 yards
Touchdowns: Walter Payton	59
RECEIVING	
Receptions: Harold Jackson	432
Yardage: Harold Jackson	7,724 yards
Per Catch Average: Mel Gray	20.0 yards
Touchdowns: Harold Jackson	61
SCORING: Jim Bakken	720 points
PUNT RETURN AVERAGE:	
Terry Metcalf	11.5 yards
KICKOFF RETURN AVERAGE:	
Terry Metcalf	26.5 yards
FIELD GOALS: Mark Moseley	152
PUNTING AVERAGE: Ron Widby	42.0 yards
INTERCEPTIONS: Paul Krause	41

DECADE LEADERS, 1970s – AFC	
PASSING	
Yardage: Ken Anderson	20,030
Completion Percentage: Ken Stabler	59.9%
Touchdowns: Ken Stabler	150
RUSHING	
Yardage: O.J. Simpson	10,539
Per Carry Average: Mercury Morris	5.2 yards
Touchdowns: Franco Harris	72
RECEIVING	
Receptions: Lydell Mitchell	374
Yardage: Ken Burrough	6,343 yards
Per Catch Average: Paul Warfield	19.9 yards
Touchdowns: Cliff Branch	50
SCORING: Jan Stenerud	875 points
PUNT RETURN AVERAGE:	
Billy "White Shoes" Johnson	13.2 yards
KICKOFF RETURN AVERAGE:	
Clarence Davis	27.1 yards
FIELD GOALS: Jan Stenerud	201
PUNTING AVERAGE: Dave Lewis	43.7 yards
INTERCEPTIONS: Jake Scott	49

Opposite: *At age 43, in 1970, George Blanda (16) of the Oakland Raiders began a five-game spree that warmed the heart of every over-the-hill, wanna-be athlete. In the sixth week of the season, he replaced an injured Darryl Lamonica at quarterback and directed the Raiders to a 31-14 victory over the Steelers. Then with :03 left against the Chiefs, he tied the game at 17-17 with a 48-yard field goal. Next, again with :03 remaining, he lifted the Raiders to a 23-20 victory over the Browns. It gets better! The following week versus the Broncos, he threw a 20-yard TD pass to Fred Biletnikoff with 2:28 remaining for a 24-19 decision. He followed that with a 16-yard field goal with :04 left to down the Chargers, 20-17. The magic left his arm and leg on Thanksgiving Day in Detroit – he couldn't rally the Raiders in a 28-14 loss to the Lions. But, by that time, America had a new folkhero. Blanda was unique. More than just a kicker, the old warrior was a viable quarterback up until the end of his 26-year career – the NFL's longest.*

Right above: *The World Football League of 1974-75 did not make much of an impact on pro football – except to raise salaries. They did break up the Miami Dolphins by signing Larry Csonka, Jim Kiick and Paul Warfield to contracts, but for the most part it was a minor league with major league aspirations. Here Chicago Fire's Mark Kellar runs the ball. October 22, 1975, became known as "the day the money ran out," and the WFL went away.*

Right below: *Blanda would not fade away after his fabled 1970 season. At age 48 in 1975, he reached another milestone. The Raiders' scoreboard tells the tale. Blanda played more years, more games, and scored more points (2,002) than anyone in the history of the pro game.*

The eighties began ordinarily enough – if you discount the Eagles defeating the Cowboys and going to Super Bowl XV, and the Oakland Raiders, as a wildcard team, defeating the Eagles for the World Championship.

The 49ers' dynasty – and in this case it isn't a word to be taken lightly – began in 1981, when they improved from 6-10 the previous year to 13-3, and went on to victory in the first non-Sun Belt Super Bowl game at Pontiac, Michigan. Mercifully, the game was played indoors.

A film entitled *My Favorite Year* played in 1982. It was not produced by Pete Rozelle. Had the NFL been involved in movie production that season, it may have chosen *The Year of Living Dangerously*. The legal action

taken by the Raiders to allow them to move to Los Angeles was settled in favor of the Raiders – and against the NFL – in 1982. After two regular season games, there was a 57-day players' strike that impacted on the playoffs and Super Bowl. And just to round out '82, the United States Football League announced it would begin play the following year. Other than the above, it was business as usual.

To fill the TV void caused by the players' strike in '82, the players union staged a mini-series of all-star games. While close in score, the games were not an artistic success, and actual paid attendance was said to have been in the mid-triple digit range.

"Replacement players" and "scabs" would become

DECADE STANDINGS – 1980s
National Football Conference

Team	W-L-T	Percentage
San Francisco 49ers[1]	104-47-1	.688
Washington Redskins[2]	97-55-0	.638
Chicago Bears[3]	92-60-0	.605
Los Angeles Rams	86-66-0	.566
New York Giants[4]	81-70-1	.536
Dallas Cowboys	79-73-0	.520
Minnesota Vikings	77-75-0	.507
Philadelphia Eagles[5]	76-74-2	.507
New Orleans Saints	67-85-0	.441
Green Bay Packers	65-84-3	.438
St. Louis/Phoenix Cardinals	62-88-2	.414
Detroit Lions	61-90-1	.405
Atlanta Falcons	57-94-1	.378
Tampa Bay Buccaneers	45-106-1	.299

[1] won NFC titles in 1981, 1984, 1988 and 1989; won SB XVI, SB XIX, SB XXIII and SB XXIV
[2] won NFC titles in 1982, 1983 and 1987; won SB XVII and SB XXII.
[3] won NFC title in 1985; won SB XX
[4] won NFC title in 1986; won SB XXI.
[5] won NFC title in 1980.

DECADE STANDINGS – 1980s
American Football Conference

Team	W-L-T	Percentage
Miami Dolphins[1]	94-57-1	.622
Denver Broncos[2]	93-58-1	.615
Oakland/Los Angeles Raiders[3]	89-63-0	.586
Cleveland Browns	83-68-1	.549
Cincinnati Bengals[4]	81-71-0	.533
New England Patriots[5]	78-74-0	.513
Seattle Seahawks	78-74-0	.513
Pittsburgh Steelers	77-75-0	.507
New York Jets	73-77-2	.487
San Diego Chargers	72-80-0	.474
Buffalo Bills	69-83-0	.454
Kansas City Chiefs	66-84-2	.441
Houston Oilers	62-90-0	.408
Baltimore/Indianapolis Colts	54-97-1	.359

[1] won AFC titles in 1982, 1984 and 1988.
[2] won AFC titles in 1986, 1987 and 1989.
[3] won AFC titles in 1980 and 1983; won SB XV and SB XVIII.
[4] won AFC titles in 1981 and 1988.
[5] won AFC title in 1985.

Pages 178-179: *Bill Walsh had been given the "genius" tag after his San Francisco 49ers won their first Super Bowl – SB XVI. Riding the shoulders of guard Guy McIntyre (62) and defensive back Mario Clark (29) after winning Super Bowl XIX in Stanford Stadium, Walsh still readily accepted all the laurels that came his way.*

Opposite top: *Perhaps no one contributed more to Bill Walsh's genius than Joe Montana (16). While at Notre Dame, Montana was noted for bringing the Irish back from the brink of defeat. He often showed the NFL that he never forgot the lessons he learned in college. After he won his first Super Bowl, the mayor of Montana's hometown was asked if they were going to name a street for him. His Honor replied, "He's already got a state named for him."*

Opposite middle: *Without Dan Marino (13), the Miami Dolphins are just another team. With the University of Pittsburgh grad, they can – and mostly do – beat anyone on any given day. Marino was part of the celebrated quarterback crop of 1983. Included were Jim Kelly, John Elway, Todd Blackledge, Tony Eason and Ken O'Brien. All were drafted before the Dolphins chose Marino as the 28th and last choice of the first round. Marino passed for more than 5,000 yards (5,084) in 1984 – the only man in NFL history to do so.*

Opposite below: *A Washington Redskins fan bites the rubber horn of a Minnesota Vikings fan after the 'Skins won the NFC Championship in January of 1988.*

part of the NFL lexicon before the decade ended. Another labor dispute, in 1987, threatened to disrupt play. Players struck, but the owners were ready – they signed replacement players or scabs, depending on where your allegiance lay, to play the scheduled games. After four weeks of such games, the regular players, sensing hopelessness, returned to work.

On the field, Walter Payton, after laboring almost single-handedly with the Bears for a decade, found himself surrounded by enough talent to be victorious in Super Bowl XX. Along the way, Payton broke Jim Brown's career rushing record and went on to gain 16,726 yards in 13 seasons.

The 49ers gave legitimacy to their claim as Team of the Decade by adding three more Super Bowl trophies to their collection – SB XIX, SB XXIII and SB XXIV.

Fans in Seattle introduced the "wave" to the NFL. This is accomplished as fans in each separate seating section consecutively rise, raise their arms, and then quickly sit down. The human undulation quickly spread east and south. Seattle fans are a notable lot. The noise they generate inside the Kingdome is legendary. Denver hates to play there – as do most teams. The Broncos practice at home the week before going to Seattle with speakers blaring crowd noise just to try to get used to what they will face. The Seahawks' management was so impressed with the advantage their fans gave the team, they retired jersey number 12 in honor of the fans – the 12th man.

With the courts ruling in favor of the Raiders' move from Oakland to Los Angeles, the league could only stand by as Robert Irsay loaded the moving vans in the middle of a 1984 spring night and took his Colts from Baltimore to Indianapolis, where they would play in the recently-constructed 61,000-seat Hoosierdome. Similarly, when the Cardinals changed zip codes – from 63188 (St. Louis) to 85001 (Phoenix) – in 1988, not much was said and even less was done.

These moves, coupled with tremendous amounts of time spent in league litigation, are thought to have prompted Commissioner Rozelle to announce his retirement in March 1989. After a bit of a struggle, Paul Tagliabue – formerly of the NFL legal team – was named commissioner.

Before leaving office, Rozelle saw yet another reversal for the NFL in the courtroom. The upstart USFL "won" its antitrust suit against the established NFL, but the victory was a hollow one: the award by the court was $1. Of course, the damage award was trebled – so the USFL had $3 with which to work, if they chose to continue play.

Where the USFL went wrong was following the suggestion of Donald Trump and a few others who wanted to compete directly with the NFL in a fall schedule and eventually force a merger with the older league. The USFL had played in 1984 and '85 as a springtime "filler" for those fans who just couldn't get enough pro football – televised or otherwise. The master plan called for no USFL football from the summer of '85 until the fall of '86, when it would go head-to-head with the NFL. After the $3 award, there was nothing for the USFL to do but disband.

The NFL finished the decade in relative calm, and looked to the nineties.

MOMENTS IN THE SUN

Super Bowl Winners of the 1980s, Each Year's Leading Passer and Where his Team Finished in League Standings.

Year/Super Bowl/Winner	Leading Passer/Team Finish
1980 – SB XV/Raiders	Brian Sipe, Browns/Won AFC Central, lost Divisional Playoff
1981 – SB XVI/49ers	Ken Anderson, Bengals/Won AFC Central, lost Super Bowl
1982 – SB XVII/Redskins★	Ken Anderson, Bengals/Third in AFC, lost in first round of playoffs
1983 – SB XVIII/Raiders	Steve Bartkowski, Falcons/Fourth (last) in NFC West
1984 – SB XIX/49ers	Dan Marino, Dolphins/Won AFC East, lost Super Bowl
1985 – SB XX/Bears	Ken O'Brien, Jets/Second in AFC East, lost AFC Wildcard
1986 – SB XXI/Giants	Dan Marino, Dolphins/Third in AFC East
1987 – SB XXII/Redskins	Joe Montana, 49ers/Won NFC West, lost Divisional Playoff
1988 – SB XXIII/49ers	Boomer Esiason, Bengals/Won AFC Central, lost Super Bowl
1989 – SB XXIV/49ers	Boomer Esiason, Bengals/Fourth (last) in AFC Central

★Strike year; regular playoff format suspended.

Opposite: *Not every quarterback can lead his team to multiple Super Bowl victories. That is not to say that some pretty good QBs haven't come close. With the Cleveland Browns, Brian Sipe (17) got about as close as you can get without going to the Super Bowl in the 1980 post-season. He was a wind-blown interception away from having his team replace the Raiders in Super Bowl XV. As it was, he settled for being NFL Player of the Year. Sipe, out of San Diego State – where he played for the air-minded Don Coryell – would have many productive years in Cleveland.*

Left above and below: *Ron Jaworski (7) came out of Youngstown State and joined the Rams in 1974. He moved to the Philadelphia Eagles in 1977, and became a local landmark. Jaworski took his team – with help from Wilbert Montgomery and others – to Super Bowl XV. But, like Sipe, Jaworski fell victim to the renegade Raiders, a wildcard team.*

Page 184: *After many frustrating years with the New England Patriots, Steve Grogan (14) finally got the team into Super Bowl XX, only to be demolished by the Bears, 46-10. Grogan, however, played long (1975-90) and well for the Pats. A gutsy field general, an effective runner, and a good enough passer to gain 3,286 yards in 1979, Grogan also led the NFL in touchdown passes that season with 28.*

Page 185: *Joe Theismann (7, handing off to John Riggins) pronounced his name "Theeze-man" until he got so good at Notre Dame that a sports information director thought it should be "Thighs-man, as in Heisman." Joe lost out to Jim Plunkett of Stanford for the Downtown Athletic Club's prized piece of bronze, but his pro career had its share of highlights. Drafted by the Dolphins in 1971, Theismann opted to play with the Toronto Argonauts of the Canadian Football League. Coming back to the USA, he was traded by Miami to the Washington Redskins for the 1974 season. So anxious was he to play, that he actually volunteered to return punts. As a fulltime quarterback, Theismann led his team to Super Bowls XVII and XVIII – winning XVII.*

FOR THE DEFENSE

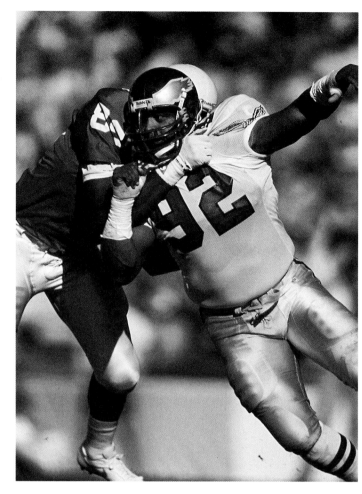

Opposite: *Randy White (54) of the Dallas Cowboys, touching down Ron Jaworski, was nicknamed "Manster" – half man, half monster – by teammate Charlie Waters. He was tried at middle linebacker with only moderate success early in his career, but became one of the very best when switched to defensive tackle.*

Above: *Michael Dean Perry (92) of the Browns, at 285 pounds, is William Perry's little brother, literally. Many will tell you he is a bigger talent than "the Fridge."*

Above right: *Reggie White (92) of the Philadelphia Eagles is often the victim of an opponent's hold, but he still plays well enough to be called the "Minister of Defense," and it's not only because he's an ordained minister. He is averaging a sack per game throughout his career, which began with the Memphis Showboats of the USFL in 1984.*

Right: *Mike Haynes was a great kick returner and cornerback for the Patriots before going to his hometown Los Angeles Raiders in 1983.*

RENEGADES AND RETREADS
The Raiders

Left above: *The Raiders – whether in Oakland, Los Angeles, or anywhere else – will tell you that there is such a thing as "the Raider way." It starts at the top with team owner Al Davis and his "just win, baby" philosophy. For years the Raiders have done it their way, taking the NFL's renegades, malcontents, "has beens," and "never wasses," and getting many productive seasons out of them. They haven't been afraid to take a chance on an unconventional player or use a draft choice in an unconventional way – more often than not, with positive results. For every Mike McCoy or Monte Jackson, there is a Ted Hendricks. For every Charles Philyaw or Eldridge Dickey, there is a Marcus Allen.*

Left below: *Probably no one fit the Raiders' outlaw image better, nor was more of a reclamation project, than Lyle Alzado (77). After the Broncos and the Browns deemed him expendable, Alzado typified the Raiders for four more years.*

Opposite: *More of a retread than a renegade, in fact there was no renegade whatever in him, Jim Plunkett (16) was just class. After wearing out his welcome – if not his arm – with the Patriots because of little support, Plunkett was traded to the 49ers. Things didn't work out there, and he was waived in August of 1978. The Raiders shrewdly signed the ex-Heisman Trophy winner, but he did not play a down that season. In 1979 he played only four games, throwing just 15 passes. It was a different tale – a Cinderella story – in 1980. Plunkett took the team, as an underdog wildcard, to Super Bowl XV, won it, and took home the MVP trophy. He would take the Raiders back to the "big dance" in January of 1984 and win again, this time defeating the Redskins, 38-9.*

Above: *Todd Christensen (46) was a first-round draft choice of the Cowboys as a fullback from BYU. He didn't make it with them, nor with the Giants, but with the Raiders he developed into an All-Pro tight end. In 1983 he made 92 catches; in '86 he had 95. Today, he is an up-and-coming network commentator.*

Left: *Marcus Allen (32), after reversing his field, is on his way to the longest scrimmage run in Super Bowl history – 74 yards against the Redskins in Super Bowl XVIII.*

Opposite: *John Matuszak (72), like Alzado, was a true Raiders renegade. He was drafted first-overall by the Oilers in 1973 out of the University of Tampa. But the 6' 8", 275-pound defensive tackle did little. He jumped to the World Football League, then to the Chiefs, on to the Redskins, and finally found refuge in Oakland in 1976. The Raiders' move to Los Angeles – with Hollywood nearby – was tailor-made for "the Tooz," who then launched a TV and film career while still playing.*

BEST EVER!?!
The Great San Diego vs. Miami Overtime Playoff in 1982

Opposite: *Chuck Muncie (46) was one of the players who helped the San Diego Chargers get off to a flying 24-0 start in the January 1982 AFC Divisional playoff game. Making the tackle is Dolphins cornerback Fulton Walker. Stopped here after a short gain, Muncie would carry the ball 24 times in the five quarters of play for 120 yards – he scored earlier on a one-yard burst.*

Above: *Football is a team sport, but if ever there was a football game that belonged to an individual – it was this game and Kellen Winslow (80). The tight end of the Chargers, who redefined the position, made a record 13 catches for 166 yards, blocked what could have been the winning field goal, and totally spent himself in five quarters as his team won, 41-38.*

Right: *Even though the Chargers got out in front 24-0, the Dolphins narrowed the gap to 24-17 at the half. Helping the comeback was Joe Rose (80), taking a scoring pass from Don Strock, who replaced starter David Woodley early on. Just before the first-half gun, Don Shula shocked the Chargers – and a national TV audience – with a daring flea-flicker play. The Dolphins would tie the score at 31-31 in the third.*

LEGENDARY LINEMEN

Opposite above and below: *Howie Long (75) of the Oakland/Los Angeles Raiders liked to tell people that his college retired his jersey. That's true, but since Villanova dropped football for seven years, they retired everyone else's too. Regardless, the handsome, articulate Long plays his position with the best of them. His position, however, is several – defensive end, defensive tackle, and nose tackle. Purely and simply, at 6' 5", 270 pounds, Howie Long is a force. He has garnered about every award a defensive lineman can. Long is the last Raider to have played in Oakland – his rookie year, 1981.*

Left above: *In high school, Gene Upshaw played for the Robstown (Texas) Cottonpickers. In college, with the Texas A&I Javelinas. He probably relished going to Oakland as a rookie in 1967 and playing for the more conventionally-named Raiders. Upshaw teamed with left tackle Art Shell – who joins him as a Hall of Famer – to give the Raiders what was called the "strongest 'weakside' (left side) in football." This was appropriate, because – led by southpaw quarterback Ken Stabler – the Raiders ran their plays to the left more often than any other team in the NFL.*

Left below: *Despite more knee operations (10) than the more publicized Joe Namath, Dan Hampton (99) played top-flight defensive end. He was a vital part of the Chicago Bears' defense that took the team to Super Bowl XX, where they destroyed the Patriots, 46-10. Hampton, called "Danimal," played a dozen years – 1979-90 – and earned Pro Bowl honors four times.*

Page 196: *Lee Roy Selmon (63) came to the expansion Tampa Bay Buccaneers in their first year (1976) as the first overall draft choice. He was an All-America and Outland Trophy winner at Oklahoma and, in the rough early going, for the Bucs a near-solitary bright spot.*

Page 197: *Steve McMichael (76) gets in the face of the Lions' Erik Kramer (12) in a 1991 game. McMichael is the middle of the Bears' line.*

THEY SHALL NOT PASS
Defensive Backs

Opposite: *If the Kansas City Chiefs' Albert Lewis (29) isn't the best cornerback in the NFL, he's second only to the Redskins' Darrell Green. That makes him the best in the AFC, at the very least. The Grambling graduate doesn't have the high interception numbers others might have, but that's because quarterbacks are reluctant to probe his sector of the field.*

Above: *Everson Walls made his reputation with the Cowboys as a free agent from Grambling, but after being signed by the New York Giants in 1990, the only man to ever lead the NFL in interceptions three times – 1981, '82 and '85 – proved he still had it.*

Right above: *Lester Hayes did as much as anyone to have the NFL ban the use of "stickum" – he slathered his arms and legs with it. With or without the sticky stuff, he was as good a "bump 'n' run" cornerback as there was in his era – 1977-86.*

Right below: *Deron Cherry made his point with the Chiefs for 11 seasons after joining the team out of Rutgers in 1981 as a free agent. He played free safety with the same style that Albert Lewis plays the corner, and that's about as good as it gets. Cherry retired just before the start of training camp in 1992 with a career total of 50 interceptions. Against the Seahawks on September 29, 1985, Cherry tied an NFL record for the most interceptions in a game, with four.*

34 + 46 = SB
Bears of the Eighties

Rushing Champions of the 1980s and Where Their Teams Finished Compared to Team Rushing Champions and Finishes				
Year	Rushing Champion-Team/Yards	Team Finish	Team Champion/Yards	Team Finish
1980	Earl Campbell-Oilers/1934	2nd in AFC Central	Saints/3106	4th (last) in NFC West
1981	George Rogers-Saints/1674	4th (last) in NFC West	Lions/2795	2nd in NFC Central
1982*	Freeman McNeil-Jets/786	6th in AFC	Bills/1371	9th in AFC
1983	Eric Dickerson-Rams/1808	2nd in NFC West	Bears/2727	3rd in NFC Central
1984	Eric Dickerson-Rams/2105	2nd in NFC West	Bears/2974	1st in NFC Central
1985	Marcus Allen-Raiders/1759	1st in AFC West	Bears/2761	1st in NFC Central, won Super Bowl XX
1986	Eric Dickerson-Colts/1821	5th in AFC East	Bears/2700	1st in NFC Central
1987	Charles White-Browns/1374	1st in AFC Central	49ers/2237	1st in NFC West
1988	Eric Dickerson-Colts/1659	2nd in AFC East	Bengals/2710	1st in AFC Central
1989	Christian Okoye-Chiefs/1480	2nd in AFC West	Bengals/2483	2nd in AFC Central

*Strike year; only 9 regular season games.

Opposite: *Walter Payton, with his jersey number 34 and Doug Plank, after whom the 46-Defense (Plank's jersey number) is named, may have helped immeasurably in getting the Chicago Bears to the Super Bowl, but the driving force behind the team's success was head coach Mike Ditka. As a player, Ditka set a new standard for tight end play with the Bears. After returning to coach the team in 1982, Ditka helped restore the Bears' Monsters of the Midway image.*

Right: *Chicago isn't called the Windy City for nothing, but the faithful brave the chilling Lake Michigan winds to root for their Bears.*

Below: *Richard Dent was drafted by the Bears, out of Tennessee State, in 1983 on the eighth round. It was a draft choice well spent. Dent became one of the best "speed rushers" in the game, peaking with being named MVP in Super Bowl XX.*

Below right: *One of the game's best linebackers, Mike Singletary was a staple of Chicago's defense. In addition, he was an All-Pro and team leader.*

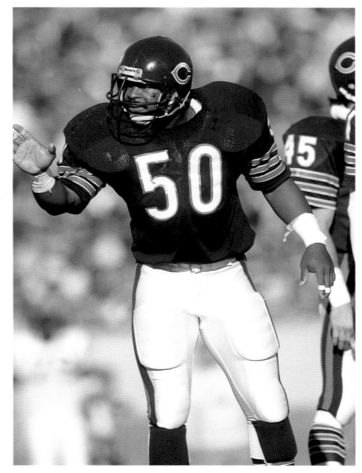

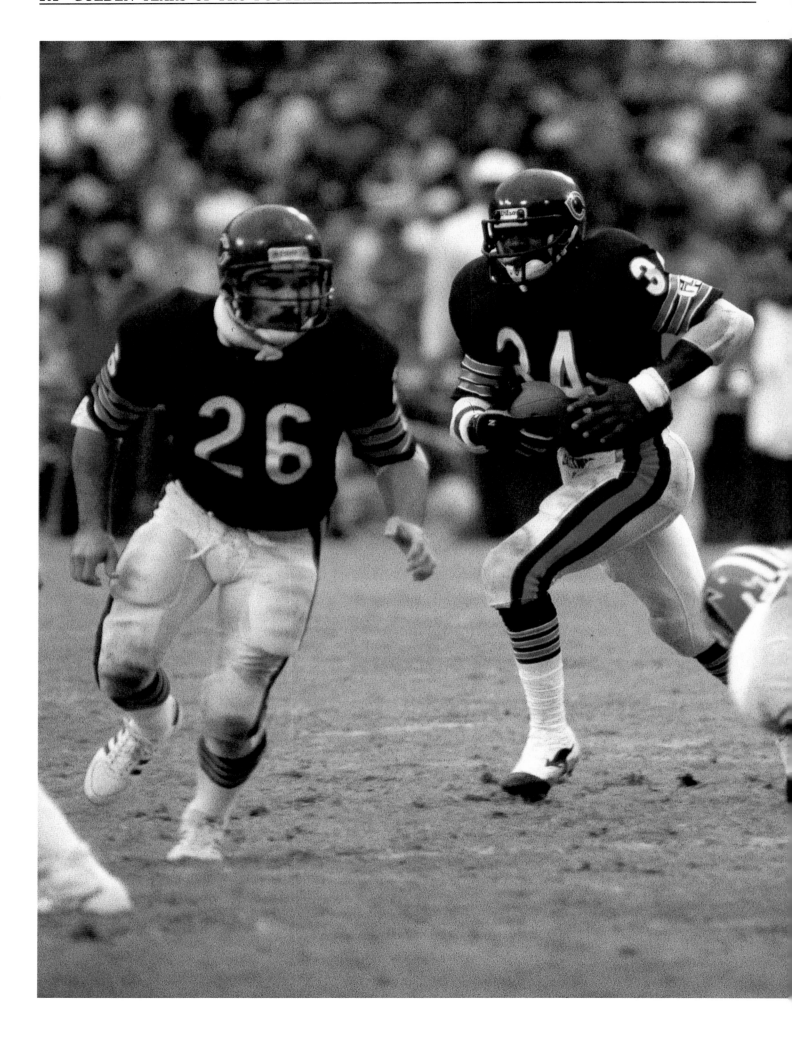

Left and Above: *Payton (left: 34, following the block of Matt Suhey, 26), came out of Jackson State in 1975 and went on to become the NFL's most productive runner. In his 13 seasons, "Sweetness" gained 16,726 yards – shattering what was thought to be Jim Brown's unbreakable career rushing record. Other runners were faster, bigger, stronger, but no one combined great ability, tremendous desire, and endurance better than the 5′ 10″, 202-pound Payton. Seldom did he fail to gain 1,000 yards a year. Only once did he miss a game in 13 years, and that moved him to tears. To put things in proper perspective – Bo Jackson missed more games in his first half-season in the NFL than Payton did in his 13 seasons. Payton struggled with some "bad news" Bears teams, but he never slacked off. His airborne touchdown dives from near the goal line were his calling card. Payton also is the Bears' leading receiver with 492 catches. When he wasn't running or catching, Payton was as good a blocker as any running back ever was. Ironically, when Payton finally got to the Super Bowl, after a decade of trial and tribulation, it was Jim McMahon and William Perry who got to take the ball into the end zone when the offense got close to the goal line. Payton is now involved in auto racing and in trying to bring an NFL expansion franchise to St. Louis.*

LITTLE BIG MEN

Left above: *In the Land of the Giants, the NFL, there are still players who don't fit the mold. As players get bigger, stronger and faster, a few come along who are throwbacks to the very beginnings of the sport – a tiny kick returner; a sawed-off nose tackle or offensive guard; a diminutive wide receiver. Sam Mills is one such throwback. The New Orleans Saints' press book lists him, generously, at 5' 9". It's good Mills is depicted here solo. Mills, who weighs 225, might look out of place beside fellow linebackers Pat Swilling (6' 3", 242 lbs.), Vaughan Johnson (6' 2", 243 lbs.), and Rickey Jackson (6' 2", 245 lbs.). From Montclair State, Mills took a circuitous route to the NFL. Signed and released early by the Browns, he experienced the same fate with Toronto of the CFL before finding a home with the Philadelphia/Baltimore Stars of the USFL. Playing for his present head coach, Jim Mora, Mills made All-USFL 1983-85. When Mora took the Saints' job in 1986, he took Sam with him. Mills has made three Pro Bowls.*

Left below: *The Atlanta Falcons' Reggie Smith (16) was listed at 5' 4", 168 pounds. This was to make him the shortest man in NFL history. But research shows that not to be so. Jack Shapiro, a halfback from NYU who played with the Staten Island Stapletons in 1929, was listed at 5' 2", 126 pounds. However, when Smith received a little notoriety as a rookie in 1980, Shapiro produced a draft registration card from World War II that had him listed at 5' ½". Smith was a serviceable kick returner for a couple of seasons.*

Opposite: *Mel Gray is 5' 9" – the same as Sam Mills – but weighs only 162 pounds. From Coffeyville J.C. and Purdue, Gray found his way to the NFL much like Mills, playing with the USFL (L.A. Express) and then the Saints. Gray was acquired by the Detroit Lions in 1989. They use him as an all-purpose speedster. In the last few years he's concentrated on punt and kickoff returns – leading the NFL in both in 1991 (punt returns average, 15.4 yards; kickoff returns average, 25.8).*

AIR CORYELL
Chargers Under Don Coryell

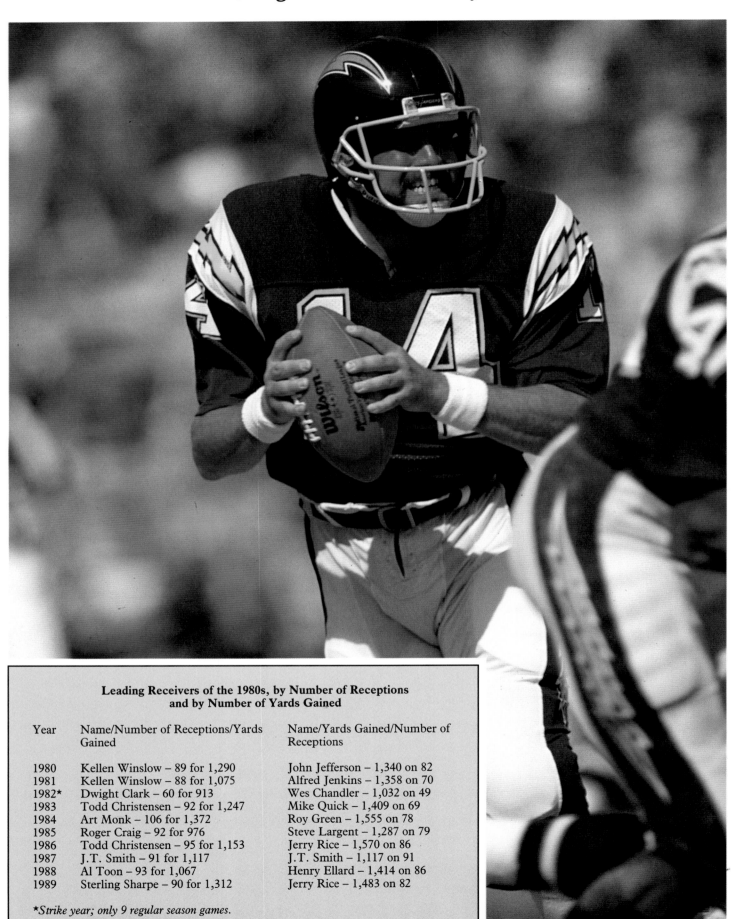

**Leading Receivers of the 1980s, by Number of Receptions
and by Number of Yards Gained**

Year	Name/Number of Receptions/Yards Gained	Name/Yards Gained/Number of Receptions
1980	Kellen Winslow – 89 for 1,290	John Jefferson – 1,340 on 82
1981	Kellen Winslow – 88 for 1,075	Alfred Jenkins – 1,358 on 70
1982*	Dwight Clark – 60 for 913	Wes Chandler – 1,032 on 49
1983	Todd Christensen – 92 for 1,247	Mike Quick – 1,409 on 69
1984	Art Monk – 106 for 1,372	Roy Green – 1,555 on 78
1985	Roger Craig – 92 for 976	Steve Largent – 1,287 on 79
1986	Todd Christensen – 95 for 1,153	Jerry Rice – 1,570 on 86
1987	J.T. Smith – 91 for 1,117	J.T. Smith – 1,117 on 91
1988	Al Toon – 93 for 1,067	Henry Ellard – 1,414 on 86
1989	Sterling Sharpe – 90 for 1,312	Jerry Rice – 1,483 on 82

Strike year; only 9 regular season games.

Opposite: *Perhaps there was never more exciting or entertaining pro football played than that practiced by the San Diego Chargers of the late seventies and early eighties. It was called Air Coryell, in honor of head coach Don Coryell, whose philosophy seemed to be, "if you score enough points, you don't have to be overly-concerned with defense." Air Coryell's ace pilot was Don Fouts (14). From Oregon, Fouts spent his rookie season, 1973, learning at the foot of the master – Johnny Unitas. He would go on to be the most dangerous deep passer of the time. He retired in 1987 with 40,040 yards – second only to Fran Tarkenton. Fouts also trails only Tarkenton in attempts (5,604) and completions (3,297). From 1979 to 1982 Fouts topped the NFL in passing yards. Fifty-one times, more than anyone else, Fouts threw for more than 300 yards in a game. Granted, he had a tailor-made offense, and a cadre of good-hands receivers, but it was Fouts who had to stand in and deliver. With few exceptions, Fouts never had the luxury of a viable running game to keep the defense honest.*

Right above: *Kellen Winslow was a wide receiver masquerading in a tight end's body (6' 5", 252 lbs.). From his tight end position, he could go deep. He simply overwhelmed smaller defensive backs. Until an injury robbed him of much of his skill, Winslow seemed to catch at will in the undermanned secondaries – a league-leading 89 and 88 in 1980 and 1981, respectively; 54 in the strike-shortened (only nine games) 1982 season; and 88 again in 1983. Then came the knee injury.*

Right below: *When John Jefferson, who could catch with anyone, held out and was traded, Wes Chandler (89) took up the slack. Teamed with Winslow and the reliable Charlie Joiner, Chandler saw to it that Air Coryell didn't miss a scheduled takeoff. To illustrate how interchangeable the parts were, in 1980, Jefferson, Winslow and Joiner all had more than 1,000 yards receiving; in '81, Chandler, Winslow and Joiner repeated the feat.*

SIDEWINDERS AND A DINOSAUR
Kickers

Opposite: *Pete Gogolak started it. He was the first soccer-style kicker to play pro football. He debuted with the Bills in 1964. By the 1980s only one straight-on kicker was left in the NFL. Matt Bahr (9) is just one of many soccer-style practitioners. Bahr is with the New York Giants after stops in Pittsburgh, Cleveland and San Francisco. Like his brother Chris, who also kicked in the NFL (1976-88), Matt played football – and soccer – at Penn State. Their father, Walter, a member of the 1950 USA World Cup soccer champions, was their coach at PSU.*

Left above: *Jan Stenerud is the first pure kicking specialist to be inducted into the Pro Football Hall of Fame – not bad for a native of Norway who came to this country on a ski-jumping scholarship at Montana State. In a storied incident Stenerud was watching football practice when a stray ball came his way. He picked it up and sent it back to the scrimmage with a kick measurably better than any of the Bobcats' players could manage. Stenerud was given a uniform – and the rest is NFL history. In 19 seasons (1967-85), Stenerud scored 1,699 points with the Kansas City Chiefs, Packers and Vikings. He is Canton, class of '91.*

Left below: *Mark Moseley was the dinosaur – the last straight-away kicker. Moseley kicked in the NFL from 1970 to 1986. He played with the Eagles (1970) and the Oilers (1971-72). He sat out 1973, and found a long-term home with the Washington Redskins in 1974. For his career, he had 1,382 points. After winning Player of the Year honors in 1982, the unassuming Moseley remarked, "I didn't even think kickers were eligible."*

Pages 210-211: *The Pittsburgh Steelers' Gary Anderson, a native of Orange Free State, South Africa, booms one past the Oilers' rush. Anderson made 229 of his first 300 NFL field goal attempts. He duels Nick Lowery and Morten Andersen for the top kicking percentage in NFL history.*

FUTURE LEGENDS
Future or Present Greats

Opposite: *Lawrence Taylor may be the best ever to have played the position of outside linebacker. As he came to the New York Giants in 1981 as a No. 1 draft choice from North Carolina, he ushered in an era where the NFL's best athletes were outside linebackers. LT played in 10 consecutive Pro Bowls.*

Above: *Offensive tackle Anthony Muñoz was the third player taken in the 1980 draft, by the Cincinnati Bengals. He merited the Bengals' confidence in his ability as he has been a fixture at left tackle ever since. He has played in eight Pro Bowls.*

Right above: *Randall Cunningham of the Philadelphia Eagles brings a new dimension to quarterbacking. Not only does he have as strong an arm as anyone in the league, he can run better than some NFL running backs. In 1990 he rushed for 942 yards – gaining 8 yards every time he ran with the ball. A punter in college (at UNLV), Cunningham was once forced to punt for the Eagles in a crucial game with the Giants. He uncorked one for 91 yards, third-longest in NFL history. A knee injury in the first game of 1991 has not dimmed his athletic brilliance.*

Right below: *Dolphins quarterback Dan Marino holds the record for the most passing yards in a season – 5,084. With his quick release, his rifle-like arm and his pinpoint accuracy, he could own all significant marks before his career ends.*

TEAM OF THE EIGHTIES
The 49ers

Super Bowl Records Set Against the Denver Broncos

SCORING – Individual
Most Points, Single Game:
18, Jerry Rice (49ers)   SB XXIV
Most PATs, Single Game:
7, Mike Cofer (49ers)   SB XXIV

RUSHING – Individual
Most Rushing Yards, Single Game:
204, Timmy Smith (Redskins)   SB XXII
Most Rushing TDs, Single Game:
2, Timmy Smith (Redskins)   SB XXII

PASSING – Individual
Most Consecutive Completions:
13, Joe Montana (49ers)   SB XXIV
Highest Completion Percentage:
88%, Phil Simms (Giants)   SB XXI
Longest Pass Completion: 80 yards,
Doug Williams (to Ricky Sanders – Redskins)   SB XXII
Most TD Passes, Single Game:
5, Joe Montana (49ers)   SB XXIV

RECEIVING – Individual
Longest Reception: 80 yards, Ricky Sanders
(from Doug Williams – Redskins)   SB XXII
Most TD Receptions: 3, Jerry Rice (49ers)   SB XXIV

COMBINED YARDAGE – Individual
Most Combined Yards, Single Game:
239, Ricky Sanders (Redskins)   SB XXII

SCORING – Team
Most Points, Single Game: 55 (49ers)   SB XXIV
Largest Margin of Victory: 45 (49ers)   SB XXIV
Most Points, First Half: 35 (Redskins)   SB XXII
Most Points, Second Half: 30 (Giants)   SB XXI
Most Points, One Quarter: 35 (Redskins,
second quarter)   SB XXII
Most Touchdowns, Single Game: 8 (49ers)   SB XXIV
Most PATs, Single Game: 7 (49ers)   SB XXIV

OFFENSE – Team
Most Total Yards: 602 (Redskins)   SB XXII
Most Rushing Yards: 280 (Redskins)   SB XXII
Highest Rushing Average Per Carry:
7.00 yards (Redskins)   SB XXII
Highest Pass Completion Percentage:
88% (Giants)   SB XXI

Opposite below: *Anytime a team wins four Super Bowls in the same decade, like the San Francisco 49ers did – winning Super Bowls XVI, XIX, XXIII and XXIV – it is likely that the team will be called the Team of the (fill in the decade). Led by Joe Montana (16), the 49ers were an eighties team. Montana put Bill Walsh's theories to work on the playing field. But the Niners' defense was stronger than most thought. And their receivers knew how to get open. Plus, Roger Craig may have been the best all-around back of the late eighties.*

Left: *Jerry Rice beats Bengals cornerback Louis Billups (24) for the Niners' first touchdown in the suspenseful Super Bowl XXIII, which the 49ers pulled out 20-16. When first-rounder Rice (80) came to town from little Mississippi Valley State in 1985, he stood the NFL's defensive backs on their collective ear. He had an immediate impact on the Walsh/Montana passing game. Starting only four games in '85, Rice still made 49 catches as a rookie – rather modest for Rice, but a number for which many an NFL wideout would hock the family jewels. From there, Rice only got better. He hit his peak, thus far, in 1990 when he pulled in an even 100 receptions. Only Art Monk and Charley Hennigan ever caught more in a season. He also tied an NFL mark in '90 for most touchdown catches in a game, with five against Atlanta. Rice has a good chance of setting new NFL receiving records in many categories before his career is ended.*

Left above: *Just as a valid argument can be made for Joe Montana being the best quarterback to have played the game, the same thing could be said for Ronnie Lott (42) being the best defensive back to ever lace up a pair of Nikes. Lott, a first-round choice out of USC in 1981, was an instant starter and played several positions, at a high level, in the defensive backfield for the 49ers over the next decade. After the 1990 season, Lott was signed as a Plan B free agent by the Raiders. He showed his game had not lost much by being the leader of the Raiders' secondary.*

Left below: *Roger Craig (33) could run, catch and block with anyone. During the pregame show before Super Bowl XIX, O. J. Simpson said on network TV that Craig "could have a big day." The Juice was right – the ex-Cornhusker fullback scored three touchdowns, on an 8-yard pass, a 2-yard run, and a 16-yard pass. Still, Joe Montana received the MVP Award as the Niners swamped the Dolphins, 38-16.*

Opposite: *Not many people heard of John Taylor (82) while he played at Delaware State in the mid-1980s, but the 49ers' personnel department knew about him – they took him on the third round in 1987. Taylor did the usual rookie things his first year, playing special teams and catching a few passes. In his second year he came to the fore as a kick returner. In his third he started opposite Jerry Rice, and the defense didn't quite know what to do or which player to cover. Taylor caught 60 balls in 1989, establishing himself as one of the game's more dangerous deep threats. Against the Rams that year, Taylor scored on TD passes of 95 and 92 yards. Since the game was a "Monday Night Football" contest, he was well on his way to becoming a household name. Neither catch was an NFL record, but it was the first time any NFL player scored from scrimmage on two 90-plus-yard touchdowns in the same game. While all this was happening, Taylor – shown spiking the ball after the winning TD in Super Bowl XXIII – was still returning kicks in deadly fashion.*

DECADE HIGHLIGHTS

DECADE LEADERS, 1980s – NFC

PASSING
Yardage: Joe Montana	30,958
Completion Percentage: Joe Montana	63.9%
Touchdowns: Joe Montana	215

RUSHING
Yardage: Walter Payton	9,800
Per Carry Average: Stump Mitchell	4.7 yards
Touchdowns: John Riggins	62

RECEIVING
Receptions: Art Monk	662
Yardage: Art Monk	9,165 yards
Per Catch Average: Willie Gault	19.8 yards
Touchdowns: Jerry Rice	66
SCORING: Eddie Murray	943 points
PUNT RETURN AVERAGE: John Taylor	12.1 yards
KICKOFF RETURN AVERAGE: Mel Gray	24.0 yards
FIELD GOALS: Eddie Murray	212
PUNTING AVERAGE: Sean Landeta	43.3 yards
INTERCEPTIONS: Ronnie Lott	48

DECADE LEADERS, 1980s – AFC

PASSING
Yardage: Dan Fouts	28,301
Completion Percentage: Ken Anderson	64.6%
Touchdowns: Dan Marino	220

RUSHING
Yardage: Marcus Allen	7,275
Per Carry Average: James Brooks	4.8 yards
Touchdowns: Marcus Allen	63

RECEIVING
Receptions: Steve Largent	595
Yardage: Steve Largent	9,336 yards
Per Catch Average: Stanley Morgan	18.6 yards
Touchdowns: Steve Largent	69
SCORING: Nick Lowery	1,006 points
PUNT RETURN AVERAGE: Louis Lipps	11.3 yards
KICKOFF RETURN AVERAGE: Rod Woodson	24.7 yards
FIELD GOALS: Nick Lowery	225
PUNTING AVERAGE: Rohn Stark	44.2 yards
INTERCEPTIONS: Dave Brown	46

Opposite: *John Riggins (44) did it his way. With the Jets, it was granny glasses, a suede vest without shirt, and a Mohawk haircut. With the Washington Redskins, it was playing past an age when most backs would have retired. He played long enough and well enough to be inducted into Canton in 1992. The Diesel, as the 235-pound workhorse was called, had back-to-back 1,000-yard seasons at ages 34 and 35 – 1,347 in 1983 and 1,239 in '84.*

Right: *Herschel Walker (34, with the New Jersey Generals of the USFL) caused a stir when he signed with the pros and passed up his senior year at Georgia after winning the Heisman as a junior. In the NFL, he played with Dallas, Minnesota and Philadelphia.*

Below: *What Doug Williams (17) of the Redskins did to the Broncos in the second quarter of Super Bowl XXII would make most QBs happy for a full game. Trailing 10-0, Williams erupted for 4 touchdown passes – 80, 27, 50, and 8 yards – as his team scored 35 points on its way to a 42-10 victory.*

Opposite: *If the Houston Oilers are to get to a Super Bowl, Warren Moon is the man to take them there. His passing stats rival those of any quarterback in the game today.*

Right: *John Hannah (73) of the New England Patriots is in the Hall of Fame with just a handful of offensive linemen. The perennial All-Pro could be the best of the bunch. No one was a more devastating run or "drive" blocker.*

Below: *William "the Refrigerator" Perry was a household name in his rookie season with the Chicago Bears as they turned him into a short-yardage blaster. However, the tackle's ballooning weight caused him to lose favor with coach Mike Ditka.*

Below right: *Jim Kelly is a Pittsburgh kid, but he didn't want to play linebacker for Joe Paterno. So, he chose Miami over Penn State and became one of a long line of Hurricane quarterbacks leaving his mark on the game. Kelly took the USFL's bigger bucks in 1984, but got to the Buffalo Bills in 1986. He has been in the upper echelon of NFL quarterbacks ever since.*

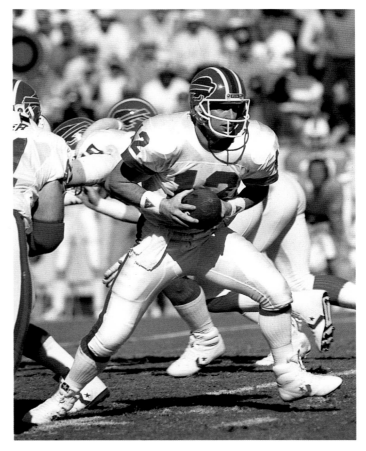

If the NFL of the eighties was "a league on the move," that motion would continue into the nineties. Thanks to strategically-placed exhibition games in London, Stockholm, Berlin, Tokyo and other cities, the NFL brand of football began to develop a worldwide following. Indeed, some claim that, aided by the world-spanning scope of NFL Properties' marketing strategy, the NFL's "stars, stripes and football" logo is second only to Coca-Cola as an internationally-recognized trademark.

With the beginning of play in the spring of 1991, the World League of American Football – since shortened to simply the World League – brought hometown teams to London, Barcelona and Frankfurt in Europe, and to Montreal in Canada. These teams – among the WLAF's strongest in the initial season – were joined by teams in the United States in New York/New Jersey (the Knights playing in Giants Stadium), Orlando, Raleigh-Durham, Birmingham, San Antonio and Sacramento. For the 1992 season, the Ohio Glory (playing in Columbus's Ohio State Stadium) replaced Raleigh-Durham.

With the blessings, and more importantly the backing, of the NFL, the World League faces many fewer obstacles than has any other start-up pro football league. The spring league's sane salary structure is the one reason many football experts feel the World League has a chance of survival. All players are signed by the league – rather than sought by individual teams – and put into a draft pool from which teams can then select. This eliminates costly bidding. All players are paid a base of $20,000 for the season; except quarterbacks are paid $25,000 and kickers, perhaps on the theory that they work less, are paid $15,000.

After the first seasons of play, many World League players received another look from the NFL, but few had an impact. However, keep this in mind. As colleges, ever so slowly, tighten academic admission requirements for "student-athletes" and become more and more disenchanted with providing a no-cost farm system for pro sports, the "development" aspects of the World League become more important. An athlete with no serious

DECADE STANDINGS – 1990s
National Football Conference

Team	W-L-T	Percentage
San Francisco 49ers	38-10-0	.791
Washington Redskins[1]	33-15-0	.687
Dallas Cowboys[2]	31-17-0	.645
New Orleans Saints	31-17-0	.645
Philadelphia Eagles	31-17-0	.645
Chicago Bears	27-21-0	.562
New York Giants[3]	27-21-0	.562
Minnesota Vikings	25-23-0	.520
Detroit Lions	23-25-0	.479
Atlanta Falcons	21-27-0	.437
Green Bay Packers	19-29-0	.395
Los Angeles Rams	14-24-0	.291
Tampa Bay Buccaneers	14-24-0	.291
Phoenix Cardinals	13-35-0	.270

[1] won NFC title in 1991 and SB XXVI.
[2] won NFC title in 1992 and SB XXVII.
[3] won NFC title in 1990 and SB XXV.

DECADE STANDINGS – 1990s
American Football Conference

Team	W-L-T	Percentage
Buffalo Bills[1]	37-11-0	.771
Kansas City Chiefs	31-17-0	.645
Miami Dolphins	31-17-0	.645
Houston Oilers	30-18-0	.625
Los Angeles Raiders	28-20-0	.583
Pittsburgh Steelers	27-21-0	.562
Denver Broncos	25-23-0	.520
San Diego Chargers	21-27-0	.437
New York Jets	18-30-0	.375
Seattle Seahawks	18-30-0	.375
Cincinnati Bengals	17-31-0	.354
Indianapolis Colts	17-31-0	.354
Cleveland Browns	16-32-0	.333
New England Patriots	9-39-0	.187

[1] won AFC titles in 1990, 1991 and 1992.

Pages 222-223: *As he has been a main cog in the Cowboys' rise from the ashes, Emmitt Smith (22, with ball) continued to blaze the trail in Super Bowl XXVII.*

Below: *Emmitt Smith became the first NFL runner to lead the league in rushing and to play on a Super Bowl champion.*

Opposite left: *Troy Aikman (8), Super Bowl MVP in '93, had a little business to conduct before "going to Disneyland." Daryl Johnston (48) offers rock-ribbed protection.*

Opposite right: *Thurman Thomas (34) and Carwell Gardner (35) express the emotions of many after the Bills' historic and heroic, Frank Reich-led, 32-point deficit comeback over the Oilers in overtime in the 1992 playoffs.*

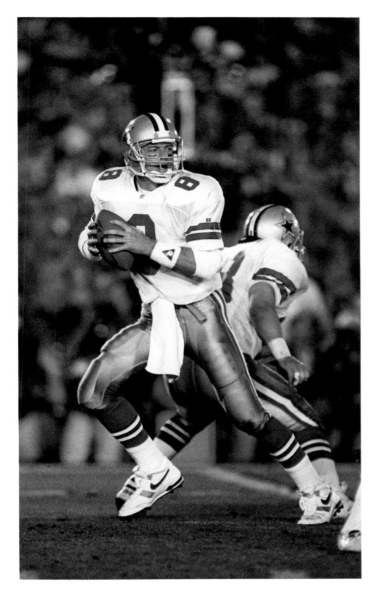

intentions for education needs a place to sharpen his skill between high school and the pros. The NFL, while trailing major league baseball, could be a jump ahead of pro basketball and some other sports.

Before the advent of the World League and the London Monarchs, England was the beneficiary of something that many in the United States longed for – a one-hour, edited version of the NFL's Game of the Week. Even the most rabid American fans may well prefer viewing an NFL game in one-third the time. The U.K.'s game of the week telecast is thought to have contributed greatly to the success of NFL preseason games and World League games played in Wembley Stadium.

In the NFL of the nineties, the NFC continues to dominate, if winning the Super Bowl is a criterion for dominance. As the decade unfolds, the NFC has won 10 of the last 12 Super Bowls – only the Raiders (of Oakland in 1981 and Los Angeles in 1984) have been able to break the NFC choke hold.

Parity, a four-letter word to some, seems to have had little adverse effect on fan interest. In fact, the opposite may be true. The average NFL stadium crowd in 1990 was 63,321. The 1990 season was noteworthy in that, for the first time since 1957, all NFL teams had won at least one of their first four games.

Fueling the flames of parity, the NFL added two more wildcard teams to the playoff mix – bringing the total to six. Add these teams to the six division winners, and you have 12 of the 28 teams making postseason play.

The player draft, with many underclassmen making up the initial picks, has also changed of late. As has the season. The television networks, in order to get another payday, negotiated for a 17-week season to play 16 games, thus giving each team an "open" Sunday. The actual televising has increased to more than just the three major "broadcast" networks – ABC, CBS and NBC. NFL football is seen on "cable" via ESPN and the Turner network (TNT).

Expansion is set for 1995, and continued growth seems to be in the long-range forecast for the NFL. Regardless of what the 21st century brings, no one can dispute that the NFL has succeeded beyond the wildest dreams of George Halas and his friends as they sat on running boards of Hupmobiles and Jordans and sipped lemonade that hot September evening in Ralph Hay's showroom on West Tuscarawas Avenue in Canton, Ohio, in 1920. And as long as teams such as the Buffalo Bills can rally from a 32-point deficit, as they did in the '92 playoffs, there is no reason to think the next century will be anything but future expansion, acceptance and growth.

NEW KIDS ON THE BLOCK

Opposite: *About the most exciting newcomer to the NFL scene recently is Barry Sanders (20) of the Detroit Lions. He understudied Thurman Thomas at Oklahoma State as a freshman, won the Heisman as a junior, and was NFL Rookie of the Year in what would have been his senior season. His NFL career has spiraled upward every year.*

Right: *Mark Rypien of the Washington Redskins signals "touchdown" in Super Bowl XXVI. He became the third Redskins quarterback of late to take the team to victory in a Super Bowl.*

Below: *If anyone can challenge Sanders for the title of "Mr. Excitement," it's the Dallas Cowboys' Emmitt Smith (22). He, as much as anyone, has brought the Cowboys back. Recruited as a Florida high school sensation by Jimmy Johnson, Smith chose the University of Florida over Miami – but all's well that ends well. Smith and Johnson are together in Big D.*

Opposite: *Eric Green of the Pittsburgh Steelers is to the '90s what Ron Kramer, Mike Ditka and John Mackey were to the '60s – the prototypical tight end. The speedy, 6', 5", 280-pounder was NFL Rookie of the Year in 1990.*

Above: *Cornelius Bennett (97) goes high to crash the Patriots' passing pocket. The 238-pound former Alabama All-America is what NFL players call "a full load." The big linebacker helped the Bills improve from a losing record to make Super Bowls XXV and XXVI.*

Right: *What Cornelius Bennett is to the Bills, Derrick Thomas (58) is to the Kansas City Chiefs. A teammate of Bennett with the Crimson Tide, Thomas is another 238-pound guided missile. Similarities continue – Thomas and Bennett are both All-Pros after being All-America in college. Both first-rounders, Bennett was the second player taken in the draft his senior year; Thomas the fourth in his.*

AROUND THE WORLD
The World League of American Football

Left: *The first president and CEO of the World League of American Football was former Dallas Cowboys president Texas E. Schramm, simply "Tex" to all who know him. Schramm, a Pro Football Hall of Famer, gave way to Mike Lynn as the World League evolved, but his guiding hand in the beginning helped.*

Below: *The stated purpose of the World League was twofold: give young players a chance to develop by playing in a springtime league, and spread the gospel – according to the NFL – to all corners of the earth. The Frankfurt (Germany) Galaxy (white jerseys) tangles with the London Monarchs in this international contest.*

Opposite: *Cheerleaders in the World League are every bit as important as they are in the NFL. Here the London "Crown Jewels" strut their stuff.*

Opposite inset: *World League Player of the Year for 1992, David Archer (18, behind the protective hulk of Ernie Rogers, 70) got a new lease on life with the Sacramento Surge. Once a starter with the Atlanta Falcons, Archer – from Iowa State – was also World Bowl II MVP.*

INTO THE NINETIES
Future Greats

Opposite above: *Timm Rosenbach (3) is the hope of the Phoenix Cardinals. With him, they are in most games. When he is hurt, as he was in 1991, the offense suffers greatly. The Washington State quarterback – he was slightly later than Mark Rypien for the Cougars – threw for 3,098 yards in 1990 after being brought along slowly as a rookie.*

Opposite below: *Like any running back, Thurman Thomas (34) of the Buffalo Bills needs some blocking – although Thomas might need less than most. He's getting great help here from All-Pro center Kent Hull (67). No one is more dangerous than Thomas running and receiving. Over a several-year span, Thomas has led the NFL in yards gained from scrimmage (rushing and receiving, combined).*

Left above: *Jeff George (11) went from Warren Central High (Indianapolis) to Purdue and then Illinois, and back again. He quarterbacks the Indianapolis Colts, and does a fine job. An overall No. 1 draft pick, he has established his credentials in just a few seasons. With a supporting cast to match his skills, George can make the Colts a contender.*

Left below: *Rod Woodson (26) does many things for the Pittsburgh Steelers. The young cornerback is already called by some the best at his position. He covers like the proverbial blanket, he tackles hard and well, and he returns punts and kickoffs with the best. In fact, he has been selected to play in the Pro Bowl, both as a kick returner and as a cornerback.*

Pages 234-235: *Forget the jewelry, the "talkin' trash," the "Prime Time" and "Neon Deion" nicknames. Remember this: Deion Sanders (21), whether playing for the Atlanta Falcons – returning a kick here against the 49ers – or with the Atlanta Braves, is a superb athlete. With the potential to star in two professional sports, Sanders can afford to play both ends against the middle.*

NEW RIDERS OF THE PURPLE SAGE
The Cowboys

Above: *Roommates and linemates with the Arkansas Razorbacks of the sixties, Jimmy Johnson (left) and Jerry Jones are head coach and owner of the Dallas Cowboys in the nineties. Under their regime, the Cowboys are closer to regaining their title of "America's Team."*

Left: *When Doug Todd was still in the Cowboys' front office, he said he was set to deal with "Aikmania." Well, Troy Aikman (8) has not yet made baby-boomer Cowboys fans forget "Beatlemania," but he could. He is generally conceded to have as much talent and ability as any young quarterback in the game today. Aikman began his career at run-oriented Oklahoma, but transferred to UCLA where he became the overall first pick in the 1989 draft.*

Opposite: *Aikman's main man for passes is Michael Irvin. He arrived big time in 1991 with 93 catches for 1,523 yards.*

ON THE HORIZON
The NFL's Newer Coaches

Left above: *Dave Shula really needs no introduction to the NFL – he's Don's son. Now the head coach of the Cincinnati Bengals, he literally grew up in the NFL. After playing high school football for Lou Maranzana at Chaminade in Hollywood, Florida, he went to Dartmouth and caught passes from Jeff Kemp for three seasons. Then it was a year with the Baltimore Colts as a wide receiver-kick returner, and on to coaching. Although only 33 when he got his first head coaching assignment, young Shula had been an NFL assistant for a decade.*

Left below: *Some call it a "rah-rah" approach; others collegiate enthusiasm. Whatever, Dennis Green brings it to the Minnesota Vikings. A head coach at academically-oriented Northwestern and Stanford, Green also had prior NFL coaching experience with the 49ers.*

Opposite above: *Rich Kotite – talking with Brad Goebel, one of many quarterbacks the Philadelphia Eagles were forced to use in 1991 when Randall Cunningham went down in the opening game – is an up-and-coming NFL head coach. Taking over for the bombastic Buddy Ryan, Kotite took his beleaguered team to within a whisker of the playoffs. Kotite, a Brooklyn native and a former sparring partner of Muhammad Ali, played tight end in the NFL with the Giants and Steelers, 1967-72.*

Opposite below: *Like Dave Shula, Bill Belichick of the Cleveland Browns has experience beyond his years. An assistant with the Colts a year after playing tight end at Wesleyan, Belichick has 18 years of NFL coaching experience behind him – and has been with the Browns since 1991. With the Giants, Belichick was credited with devising the team's leak-proof defense.*

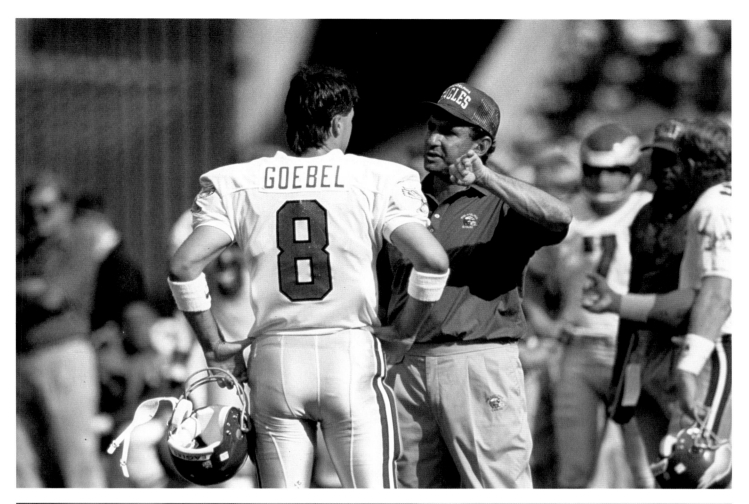

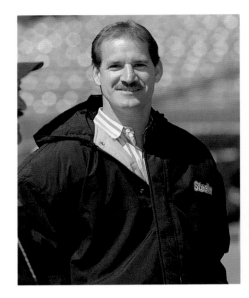

Above: *Bill Cowher, a Pittsburgh native, is meeting the challenge of a lifetime. He replaced the legendary, four-time Super Bowl winner Chuck Noll in 1992. Cowher, who played at North Carolina State, was primarily a special teams linebacker in the NFL – Browns and Eagles, 1980-84. He began coaching in 1985 and came to the Steelers after being Kansas City's defensive coordinator.*

Right: *Dick MacPherson (in blue sweater) led his New England Patriots with as much enthusiasm and youthful vigor as any of the younger head men. Best known for his work as coach of the Syracuse Orangemen, Coach Mac was no stranger to the NFL before joining the Pats in 1991. Between stints in college, he was an assistant with the Broncos (1967-70) and the Browns (1978-80). He was also head coach at Massachusetts. A combination of MacPherson's illness, a poor won-lost record and unsettled team management led to Coach Mac's dismissal after the 1992 season.*

STILL DANGEROUS AFTER ALL THESE YEARS
Veteran Performers

Opposite and Inset: *Art Monk (81) and "Ol' Man River" keep on rolling along. After a dozen years or more, the Washington Redskins' wideout has become the NFL's all-time reception leader. Monk also set a still-standing NFL record for the most receptions in a season with 106 in 1984. The 6' 3", 210-pound ex-Syracuse Orangeman is a fine downfield blocker, too. When taken in the first round of the 1980 draft by the 'Skins, it marked the first time since 1968 that Washington had and used a first-round draft choice.*

Right and Below: *Steve DeBerg (17) has made a 15-year NFL career of being the right guy at the wrong place. Out of San Jose State, he joined the 49ers and set a record in his second fulltime season for pass attempts (578), and then along came Joe Montana. He went to Denver just ahead of John Elway's debut and to Tampa Bay when the Buccaneers drafted Vinny Testaverde. DeBerg had success, most recently, with the Kansas City Chiefs, showing much courage in taking the team to the playoffs, despite a broken finger.*

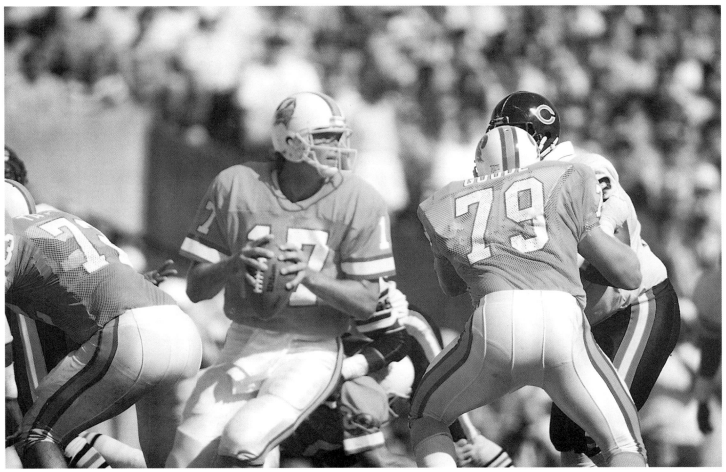

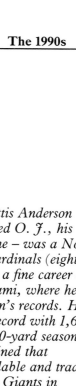

Opposite above: *Ottis Anderson (24) – sometimes called O. J., his middle name is Jerome – was a No. 1 draft choice of the Cardinals (eighth overall) in 1979 after a fine career at the University of Miami, where he broke Chuck Foreman's records. He set a rookie rushing record with 1,605 yards. After five 1,000-yard seasons, the Cardinals determined that Anderson was expendable and traded him to the New York Giants in mid-1986. He was used sparingly, and had only six yards rushing in 1987. In 1989 Joe Morris injured his foot, and the 32-year-old Anderson responded marvelously. He gained 1,023 yards in the regular season, won Comeback Player of the Year honors, and topped it off with a demonstration of ball-control running in Super Bowl XXV (102 yards and MVP honors) as the Giants edged the Bills, 20-19. Anderson is one of the top 10 rushers in NFL history.*

Opposite below: *James Lofton (80) is another ageless marvel. Shown taking a pass in Super Bowl XXV, Lofton began his career with the Packers in 1978, fresh off "the Farm" – Stanford University. He was the sixth player taken in that year's draft. After nine seasons, the Pack turned to a youth movement and Lofton found himself back in his hometown, Los Angeles, with the Raiders. Waived by the Raiders, a reclamation project Al Davis gave up on too soon, Lofton joined the Buffalo Bills for the 1989 season. He caught only eight balls that year, but three went for touchdowns. In the next two seasons, he and the Bills went to the Super Bowl. Lofton's contribution was a two-year total of 92 catches for 1,784 yards and 12 TDs. Often, when a "vintage" athlete is described, the old adage "Like fine wine, he gets better with age" is used. With James Lofton, it rings true.*

Left: *Lofton (80) of the Bills goes skyward for a pass from Jim Kelly in Super Bowl XXVI.*

LOOKING AHEAD

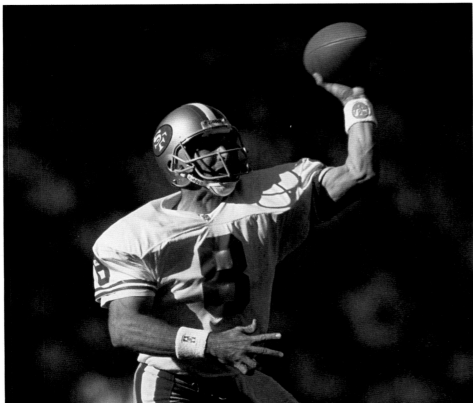

Opposite: *Barry Foster was a Steelers fifth-rounder in the 1990 draft, who gained notoriety as a rookie by watching a loose ball bound into the end zone for an opponents' touchdown. All he did in 1992 was lead the Steelers back to the playoffs and gain 1,690 yards – second-best (by a scant 23 yards) in the NFL.*

Left above: *Sterling Sharpe of the Packers could be happy about several things – finally being recognized as one of the best receivers in the league, setting the single-season record in 1992 with 108 catches, or simply scoring a touchdown.*

Left below: *Steve Young of the 49ers, again filling in for an injured Joe Montana, was the only 1992 NFL passer with a rating index of more than 100 (107.0). Some in the Bay Area feel he is still destined to live in Montana's considerable shadow.*

Above: *The intense look on coach Bobby Ross's face could be caused in part by the Chargers' four season-starting losses. He lightened up somewhat as the team won 11 of the last 12 games and made the 1992 playoffs.*

Pages 248-49: *Michael Irvin (88), who just scored in Super Bowl XXVII, and Alvin Harper (80) typify the talent and exuberance of the NFL's youngest, and possibly best, team – the Dallas Cowboys, World Champions.*

DECADE HIGHLIGHTS

Left: *Joe Gibbs of the Washington Redskins was generally acknowledged as the NFL's best coach at the time of his unexpected retirement in March 1993. Gibbs, who played at Cerritos J.C. and at San Diego State, was an assistant with the Cardinals, Buccaneers and Chargers. Gibbs took over the Redskins in 1981, and brought them to four Super Bowls, winning three. He won SB XVII with Joe Theismann at quarterback, SB XXII with Doug Williams, and SB XXVI with Mark Rypien.*

Opposite above: *John Elway (7) of the Denver Broncos is remembered by some for three sub-par Super Bowl appearances, but in Denver many still choose to remember "the Drive." In the ultimate two-minute drill, Elway led the Broncos on a 15-play, 98-yard drive to tie the score at 20-20 at the end of regulation in a January 1987 conference playoff game with the Browns. Later in the game he engineered the drive that led to Rich Karlis's winning 33-yard field goal and a Super Bowl berth.*

Opposite below: *Andre Reed (83) of the Buffalo Bills gets his team on the scoreboard after trailing the Jets, 14-0, in this 1990 game. From Pennsylvania's Kutztown University, Reed is one of the NFL's most productive receivers.*

DECADE LEADERS, 1990s – NFC

PASSING
Yardage: Jim Everett	10,750
Completion Percentage: Steve Young	65%
Touchdowns: Jim Everett	66

RUSHING
Yardage: Barry Sanders	4,204
Per Carry Average: Randall Cunningham	7.31 yards
Touchdowns: Emmitt Smith	39

RECEIVING
Receptions: Jerry Rice	264
Yardage: Jerry Rice	3,909 yards
Per Catch Average: Michael Irvin	17.9 yards
Touchdowns: Jerry Rice	37
SCORING: Chip Lohmiller	400 points
PUNT RETURN AVERAGE: Kelvin Martin	12.1 yards
KICKOFF RETURN AVERAGE: Mel Gray	24.2 yards
FIELD GOALS: Chip Lohmiller	92
PUNTING AVERAGE: Harry Newsome	44.2 yards
INTERCEPTIONS: Audray McMillan	15

DECADE LEADERS, 1990s – AFC

PASSING
Yardage: Warren Moon	11,900
Completion Percentage: Warren Moon	62.5%
Touchdowns: Jim Kelly	80

RUSHING
Yardage: Thurman Thomas	4,191
Per Carry Average: Thurman Thomas	4.8 yards
Touchdowns: Thurman Thomas	30

RECEIVING
Receptions: Haywood Jeffires	264
Yardage: Haywood Jeffires	3,142 yards
Per Catch Average: James Lofton	18.0 yards
Touchdowns: Ernest Givins	24
SCORING: Nick Lowery	356 points
PUNT RETURN AVERAGE: Rod Woodson	11.0 yards
KICKOFF RET. AVE.: Jon Vaughn	23.7 yards
FIELD GOALS: Pete Stoyanovich	82
PUNTING AVERAGE: Rohn Stark	43.6 yards
INTERCEPTIONS: Gill Byrd	17

Opposite: *Jeff Hostetler (15) of the New York Giants came from the same spawning grounds as NFL legends George Blanda, Johnny Unitas, Joe Namath, Joe Montana and Dan Marino – the mine and mill towns of Western Pennsylvania. Not wanting to become a linebacker at Penn State, where his brothers also played, Hostetler transferred to West Virginia University. He was in his fifth season with the Giants, who drafted him third in 1985, when he got his first real playing time. Starter Phil Simms went down and the Hoss replaced him late in the season, taking the Giants into the NFC Championship Game and winning Super Bowl XXV.*

Right above: *Perhaps no athlete, with the possible exception of the NBA's Michael Jordan, received more publicity and exposure than Bo Jackson, here in jersey No. 34 pursuing his "hobby" as a Los Angeles Raiders running back. Jackson gained almost 1,000 yards in his abbreviated season of 1989 – 950 yards. Jackson was originally the first player taken – by Tampa Bay – after winning the Heisman Trophy at Auburn. He chose to sign a baseball contract and forego the NFL. Eligible for the next year's draft, Jackson was taken by that sly old fox, Al Davis, on the seventh round. Like many of Davis's decisions, it was a good one. Jackson began his NFL career in 1987 by playing seven games for the Raiders late in the season, after finishing his baseball duties with the Kansas City Royals. In a 1991 post-season game against the Bengals, Jackson sustained what was thought to be a minor hip injury. It didn't come around and Jackson found himself cut loose by the Royals and subsequently signed by the Chicago White Sox.*

Right below: *Mike Utley became a symbol of courage to the nation in 1991 and a rallying point for his Detroit Lions teammates. After sustaining a paralyzing neck injury, Utley gave his concerned teammates the "thumbs up" sign as he was taken off the field. Dedicating their season to Utley, the Lions went all the way to the NFC title game.*

INDEX
Numerals in *italics* indicate photos

ACKNOWLEDGMENTS

The author and publisher would like to thank the following people who have helped in the preparation of this book: Barbara Thrasher, who edited it; John Bowman, who helped plan it; Don Longabucco, who designed it; Sara Dunphy, who did the picture research; and Jennifer Cross, who prepared the index.

PHOTO CREDITS

All photographs courtesy UPI/Bettmann Newsphotos, except the following:
Allsport: pages 189, 199 (top left). Vernon & John Biever/Allsport: pages 4-5. Dave Black/Allsport: page 199 (bottom). Melanie Carr/Allsport: page 207 (bottom). Rich Clarkson/Allsport: page 100 (top). Chris Cole/Allsport: page 230 (bottom). Jim Commentucci/Allsport: pages 229 (top), 233 (top), 239 (bottom). Jonathan Daniel/Allsport: pages 187 (top left), 188 (top), 197, 202-203 (left). Tim Defrisco/Allsport: pages 198, 251 (top). Tony Duffy/Allsport: page 212. Stephen Dunn/Allsport: pages 6-7, 194 (top), 213 (top right), 229 (bottom), 244 (bottom left), 247 (below), 248-49. Otto Greule Jr./Allsport: pages 226, 234-235, 247 (top left), 253 (bottom). Jim Gund/Allsport: pages 204 (top), 220. Ron Haase/Allsport: page 187 (bottom). Rod Hanna/Allsport: page 124. B. Hazelton/Allsport: page 188 (bottom). Bill Hickey/Allsport: page 252. T.G. Higgins/Allsport: pages 181 (center), 213 (bottom). Caryn Levy/Allsport: page 238 (top). Joe Patronite/Allsport: page 237. Doug Pensinger/Allsport: page 227 (bottom). Mike Powell/Allsport: pages 187 (top right), 190 (top), 194 (bottom), 206, 221 (bottom left), 224, 227 (bottom), 232, 243 (top), 253 (bottom). George Rose/Allsport: page 213 (top left). Dan Smith/Allsport: page 231 (left). Allen Dean Steele/Allsport: page 236 (top). Rick Stewart/Allsport: pages 205, 207 (top), 208, 222-23, 225 (both), 232 (bottom), 233 (bottom), 236 (bottom), 238 (bottom), 244 (top left), 244-245 (center), 251 (bottom). Damian

Strohmeyer/Allsport: pages 210-211, 239 (top), 241.
AP/Wide World Photo: pages 192, 193 (bottom).
Vernon J. Biever: page 66 (bottom).
Chance Brockway: pages 10 (left), 99, 111 (both), 114, 115 (bottom left), 121 (top, bottom right), 127, 131, 145 (bottom right), 149 (bottom left), 150 (top right, bottom left), 151, 156, 157 (top), 167 (both), 173 (bottom left), 201 (bottom left, right), 209 (top), 216 (top), 243 (bottom).
Jim Campbell: page 150 (bottom right).
Courtesy Chicago Bears: page 66 (top).
Scott Cunningham/Washington Redskins: page 250.
Malcolm Emmons: pages 10 (right), 92 (bottom), 98 (bottom right), 100 (bottom), 101, 110 (both), 120, 122, 126 (bottom), 136, 142 (both), 143 (top), 144, 145 (top), 157 (bottom), 158, 160, 161, 163 (top), 166, 173 (bottom right), 175 (bottom right), 176, 183 (top), 184, 186, 190 (bottom), 195 (bottom), 196, 199 (top right), 200, 209 (bottom), 214 (bottom left), 216 (bottom), 218, 219 (bottom), 221 (top right), 221 (bottom right), 242 (both).
Nancy Hogue: pages 2, 11, 132-133, 137 (both), 138, 139, 143 (bottom left), 149 (top right), 149 (bottom right), 150 (top left), 181 (top), 182, 183 (bottom), 191, 203 (top right), 204 (bottom).
Courtesy Los Angeles Raiders: page 195 (top).
Courtesy Los Angeles Rams: page 57 (top).
Courtesy NBC-TV: page 60 (top).
Courtesy New York Giants: pages 41 (bottom), 44 (bottom right).
Courtesy Pittsburgh Steelers: pages 52, 62.
Michael Fabus/Pittsburgh Steelers: pages 135 (bottom), 228, 240 (top left), 246.
Courtesy San Diego Chargers (Sam Stone): 247 (top right).
Pro-File Collection: pages 14, 17 (top), 177 (top).
Pro Football Hall of Fame: pages 9, 67 (top left and right).
Robert Riger: page 75 (top).
Anna Weaver: page 231 (bottom right).
Bob Yerger: page 69.